DECONFEDERATION

DECONFEDERATION

CANADA WITHOUT QUEBEC

David Jay Bercuson
Barry Cooper

KEY PORTER BOOKS

Canadian Cataloguing in Publication Data

Bercuson, David Jay, 1945-
    Deconfederation: Canada without
Quebec

ISBN 1-55013-356-X

1. Quebec (Province) - History - Autonomy
and independence movements. 2. Federal
government - Canada. I. Cooper, Barry,
1943-   . II. Title.

FC2925.9.S4B47 1991   971.4'04
C91-094270-6
F1053.2.B47 1991

Key Porter Books Limited
70 The Esplanade
Toronto, Ontario
M5E 1R2

Design / Maher Design

Printed and bound in Canada

91 92 93 94 95 6 5 4 3 2 1

CONTENTS

A la mémoire de
René Lévesque

PREFACE

t is time for a frank discussion on the past, present, and future of Canada and Quebec. This book is our contribution to what needs to be a national debate, couched in realistic terms, unclouded by emotionalism or diplomatic double-talk and euphemism. Events that have transpired in Canada since the death of the Meech Lake Accord on June 23, 1990, have proven to us that the Canadian experiment has failed. That experiment attempted to accommodate the special aspirations of one large minority — francophone Quebeckers — within the confines of a single liberal democracy constituted by immigrants of varied and diverse background — including the French themselves.

There is nothing unique about this conclusion; René Lévesque came to the same judgement when he wrote *Option Québec* in 1968 and founded the Mouvement souveraineté-association. Lévesque was right. Canada cannot survive when French-speaking and English-speaking Canadians relate to each other like two scorpions in a bottle. It is time to break the bottle, allow the scorpions to escape, and rebuild what is left. As in a divorce between two long-married people, the pain of separation will eventually give way to hope for a better future for both. We believe this is true of Canadians and Québécois.

We have come to this conclusion from two different starting points. Cooper is a fourth-generation Albertan. He grew up in western Canada where learning French was expected of an educated citizen — but then so was learning Latin. As with many westerners, the historical experience of many and diverse immigrants — the experience of making a fresh start in a new land, of distance from central Canada and all its political and social concerns — laid the foundations for his basic belief in the soundness of liberal democracy. As a young academic, Cooper lived and taught in Quebec and Ontario. He was an admirer and supporter of Lévesque and the Parti Québécois. He was deeply impressed by their honesty, their integrity, and their courage. He was less impressed by their appeal to Quebec emotionalism — but then as a westerner he had difficulty relating to the message. At the time he was neither a supporter nor an opponent of official bilingualism; he did believe it was beside the point.

Cooper's views on the Canada-Quebec question were also shaped by his approach to the study of politics. As a political philosopher, the principles of liberal democracy are central to his way of thinking about politics. In observing Canada's ongoing constitutional struggles over the last few years, he came to the conclusion that Canada's liberal-democratic regime has come under intolerable pressures that cannot be relieved under the present constitutional structure.

Bercuson was born and raised in anglophone Montreal. Having lived under the yoke of Duplessis, he and many other liberal-minded anglos strongly supported the Quiet Revolution. He loudly cheered René Lévesque when he came to Sir George Williams University in the fall of 1962 to put the case for the nationalization of Quebec's private power companies to these students from Westmount Rhodesia. It was also natural that he would support the young Pierre Elliott Trudeau and his bilingual vision of Canada. He worked hard for Trudeau in the 1968 federal election.

In 1970 Bercuson trekked west. There he saw a different Canada from the one he grew up in. He still strongly supported bilingualism as a measure to make Quebeckers feel at home in the rest of Canada. But by the mid-1980s he had become distressed at the efforts of the provincial premiers — not the least of whom were Alberta's Peter Lougheed and his successor, Don Getty — to create ten nations out of one. The Meech Lake process proved to him that Canada, or what was left of it, could be saved only if Quebec was allowed to go its own way.

Both of us now are prepared to advocate the total separation of Quebec from Canada. It is a far better solution to the problems that ail Canada than any other yet proposed. In fact, given historical realities, it is the only solution. We will be attacked in many quarters as "red-necked" Albertans trying to wipe French off our cereal boxes, restore the Imperial gallon, and force a single Anglo-Saxon culture down the throats of all immigrants. That is simply not true. We regret that the Canadian experiment has failed, but we would regret still more the failure of Canadians (French- and English-speaking) to realize that they are in an endless dance with the devil and that the music must end. Someone must shoot the piano player. If our readers choose to shoot us in return, so be it.

David Jay Bercuson
Barry Cooper

ACKNOWLEDGMENTS

I n writing a book such as this we have relied upon the work of other scholars, and on journalists' stories and media accounts, as well as on our own interpretations and arguments. Of course, our sources are not responsible for the use we have made of their work, but courtesy and common-sense require us to acknowledge their assistance.

In addition to newspaper reports and magazine accounts, we have relied upon the following authorities: *The Gallup Report*; Robert L. Mansell and Ronald C. Schlenker, "An Analysis of the Regional Distribution of Federal Balances: Updated Data," (Calgary, 1990); Rainer Knopff, "Democracy vs. Liberal Democracy: The Nationalist Conundrum," *Dalhousie Review*, 58:4 (Winter, 1978-79), 638-46; Rainer Knopff, "Language and Culture in the Canadian Debate: The Battle of the White Papers," *Canadian Review of Studies in Nationalism*, vi:1 (Spring, 1979), 66-82; Rainer Knopff, "Liberal Democracy and the Challenge of Nationalism in Canadian Politics," *Canadian Review of Studies in Nationalism*, ix:1 (Spring, 1982) 23-92; Donald J. Savoie, *The Politics of Public*

Spending in Canada, (Toronto, 1990); Katherine A. Graham, ed., *How Ottawa Spends: 1990-91,* (Ottawa, 1990), and previous publications in this series sponsored by the Carleton University School of Public Administration; Hubert Guindon, *Quebec Society: Tradition, Modernity and Nationhood,* (Toronto, 1988); Peter Brimelow, *The Patriot Game,* (Toronto, 1986); Janet Ajzenstat, *The Political Thought of Lord Durham,* (Kingston & Montreal, 1988); Jacques Brossard, *Le Territoire québécois,* (Montreal, 1970); Jacques Brossard, *L'Accession à la souveraineté et le cas du Québec,* (Montreal, 1976); Henri Brun, ed., *Le Territoire du Québec,* (Quebec City, 1974); William D. Gairdner, *The Trouble With Canada,* (Toronto, 1990); Alfred Oliver Hero, Jr., and Louis Balthazar, eds., *Contemporary Quebec and the United States,* (Cambridge, MA, 1988); William Shaw, Lionel Albert, *Partition: The Price of Quebec's Independence,* (Montreal, 1980); Harvey Mansfield, Jr., *The Spirit of Liberalism,* (Cambridge, MA, 1982); Dale C. Thompson, *Jean Lesage and the Quiet Revolution,* (Toronto, 1984); René Lévesque, *Memoirs,* (Toronto, 1986); Ramsay Cook, *Canada and the French Canadian Question,* (Toronto, 1966); William D. Coleman, *The Independence Movement in Quebec: 1945-1980,* (Toronto, 1984); Claude Morin, *Quebec versus Ottawa: The Struggle for Self-Government, 1960-1972,* (Toronto, 1976); Frank H. Underhill, *The Image of Confederation,* (Toronto, 1964); Robert Bothwell, John English, Ian Drummond, *Canada Since 1945,* (Toronto, 1980).

INTRODUCTION

I n the bedrooms and boardrooms of the nation, in bar-
rooms and locker-rooms, in kitchens and on the CBC,
Canadians are asking themselves: What's wrong with this
country, eh?

In one way or another the answer is always the same. At
the centre of the current crisis of Canadian political life is Quebec. The crisis has many dimensions: constitutional, economic,
linguistic, social, ethnic, cultural. Accordingly there are many
ways to talk about it. The Parti Québécois says the status quo is
intolerable and that a package deal — independence plus a
common market — is the solution; the federalists in Ottawa and
Quebec say the status quo is intolerable and that the solution is
the preservation of Canada by a renewed federalism. "The cup is
half-full," say the federalists. "No, it is half-empty," say the
indépendantistes. We say the cup is full of holes; it leaks; it's
nearly dry. The solution is two new cups.

This is not a new idea. For the best part of a generation serious and thoughtful men and women have demanded that Quebec separate from Canada. And even prior to Confederation
responsible intellectual and political leaders in Quebec thought

I

the French of North America should or must become an independent national state or face slow but inevitable extinction as a distinct people. Some gloried in the name of separatists. Others have found it an insult, a distortion, a piece of propaganda designed to frighten the timid and befuddle the resolute. Oh no! They preferred to speak of independence, or sovereignty. Or perhaps sovereignty-association. Or maybe just association with a touch of independence. Or sovereignty. Who knows?

We would like to be clear and unambiguous in our advocacy. At one time we thought Quebec and Canada could exist as a single country. But no more. At one time we thought the Constitution of 1982 was an adequate, though far from perfect, founding document. No longer. We now realize that Canada is at the end of a thirty-year constitutional crisis. If Canada were not now also facing a real and pressing economic crisis, Canadians might enjoy another thirty years of constitutional wrangles. But that is a luxury Canada can no longer afford. As we will argue, the constitutional crisis and the economic crisis are bound together, prisoners on the same chain gang. We believe that both may be met at once, but we may be mistaken. We know, however, that neither has been seriously discussed to date. This book is our response to a problem not of our making but one that all Canadians can no longer ignore.

In simple and distinct terms, we are very much in favour of the independence of Quebec. We are for the sovereignty of Quebec. We would like Quebec to be a distinct state and not merely a distinct society like British Columbia or northern Ontario. We wish Canada-Quebec relations to be under the purview of the Department of External Affairs. Can we be more clear? We wish to regard Quebec as a foreign state, like Spain or Australia or Zaire or the United States. And, as with Spain or Australia, we expect our relations to be conducted amicably, harmoniously, and in a spirit of mutual trust, respect, and goodwill.

It has become normal to hear Quebeckers assert the inevitability of independence — of the achievement of statehood — to express the organizational requirements of the nation. Nowadays even non-Quebeckers are telling phone-in shows that independence for Quebec is inevitable. But nothing has happened. There is whining and complaining and bickering. There are royal commissions and task forces and first ministers' conferences. But Quebec is still part of Canada. So we wonder: where is the inevitability? Where is the one-way street to sovereignty that René Lévesque talked about with such confidence twenty-five years ago? For twenty-five years some Canadians have been waiting to wish Quebec well and nothing has happened. Not too long ago Quebec's greatest sociologist, Hubert Guindon, offered an explanation: Quebec decided some time after the 1980 referendum that independence was a threat, not a goal.

This theme was picked up by the federalist politicians from Ottawa, from Quebec City, and from other provinces too. But it has no credibility. The independence of Quebec can only be a goal — for Quebeckers, for us, for all persons of goodwill. It never was a threat, save to those politicians and bureaucrats who feed off the current malaise. For most Canadians the independence of Quebec poses no threat to anything. The bitter and narrow-minded bigots who inhabit various holes and corners across the land will say: good riddance! The more realistic and generous will see independence as an opportunity for economic improvement and for the creation of a genuinely harmonious constitution in Canada. Besides, we know full well where taking the pseudo threat of independence seriously has landed us: in a generation-long constitutional crisis, probably the longest-running constitutional crisis in the history of the world. With luck that crisis broke in the climax of indecision called Meech Lake. Now we have a real opportunity for change — and change for the better.

Today, many Canadians — well over half according to some accounts — are ready to cut the bonds that have kept us all, Quebeckers and non-Quebeckers alike, tied together. But the Quebec ship of state is still firmly moored to the dock. The Blue Peter has been run up the mast for a quarter of a century and no one has weighed anchor. We are saying it is time to cast off. We say it with no rancour and without condescension. We propose no challenge — except to pusillanimous politicians. The last thing we wish to say is "Put up or shut up."

It very nearly goes without saying that we wish Quebec to live up to its potential as an independent state. Very nearly, because there are tender-hearted Canadians, in Quebec and elsewhere, who might view our argument as a rejection of Quebeckers, as a rejection of our fellow human beings, as some kind of personal insult. And that, too, is part of our problem: it is difficult in Canada to discuss politics seriously. We are so captivated by outdated myths and buffaloed by the thought of hurt feelings and hard feelings that we never say what we mean. So, to be clear, we are talking about politics, public affairs, and the common weal, not personal relationships, not how we feel about things, not whether we "care" about Quebec. We wish to dispel myths, not create new ones or try to revive those long dead. We are not unmindful of the economic costs of separation, at least over the short term. But we are confident that business can take care of its own interests. In recent years business has not been the problem anyway. The problem has been government and those whose interests are tied to government. More precisely, the problem has been a continuing disagreement over the ground rules of political life in Canada. This ongoing crisis over the Constitution concerns the principles by which we govern ourselves.

Our primary concern is with those principles, not with the logistics of government or with how we conduct our commercial affairs. Let us be clear at least about one thing: our intentions are not first of all practical. Of course, there are practical implications, but we desire chiefly to be clear about what Canadians have done and what it means. This is an aim modest enough to enable us to avoid one of the besetting problems of many professors (and we are both professors), namely, that they are slightly schizoid. They think they are other people, usually the president of a huge corporation or the prime minister. That is why they assert their deeply held opinions with such vehemence. That is why they offer their advice so freely. Many professors are quite certain about what to do with the economy or the foreign policy of the nation or about the hole in the ozone or the location of a dam or a pulp mill. At this point, we would simply like to shed some light on a perplexing problem. We have every confidence that business and political leaders in Canada and Quebec can work out the practical accommodations without our help.

Responsible discussion of politics involves analysis of political interests. This is the dirty little secret every politician knows but has taken a solemn oath never to reveal or discuss. Canadians are grown-up citizens, not babes from whom secrets must be hid. So when we advocate a prosperous and independent Quebec we do so not from magnanimity and benevolence alone (though, like all Canadians, we like to think of ourselves as magnanimous and benevolent), but from the high regard we have for so much of the social and cultural life of Quebec. And we are not at all prepared to sacrifice our friendships with Quebeckers. We want a separate Quebec because it is in the interests of Canadians as well as in the interests of Quebeckers.

It is sometimes forgotten that Canadians have interests at all. Well, we do. And they are not well served by the current constitutional regime. A glance at the nation's books reveals this with great clarity. The question is: what is to be done? How to break the logjam? Here goodwill and national interest push in the same direction. We do not say that the separation of Quebec will be painless or simple. But we do say it can be done in an orderly and legal way. We are sure that Canada and Quebec can be good neighbours instead of squabbling in-laws.

In less metaphorical language, we believe that Canada is a liberal democracy, and that liberal democracies are fundamentally decent regimes. But Canada is being seriously challenged both in its liberalism and in its democratic foundation by a new kind of nationalism based on ethnic and cultural characteristics and centred in the Province of Quebec. (For the purpose of this discussion we will call this Quebec nationalism or French nationalism.) The solution is not to continue a futile process of constitutional accommodation. The demands of Quebec's ethnic and cultural nationalism are simply incompatible with the continued existence of Canada as a liberal democracy. The continued attempts to meet the demands of the Province of Quebec within Canada have imperilled the entire political order of the country and contributed significantly to our current economic and social disorders. To restore the economic and political health of Canada, Quebec must leave. In this book we will discuss the historical, political, and philosophical reasons why we believe this is so.

Unfortunately, the very terms of the discussion are ambiguous: What is Quebec? Who is a Quebecker? Who is a Canadian? What is Canada? What is liberal democracy? Indeed, what is ethnic and cultural nationalism?

When we refer to Quebec as it exists under the present constitutional regime, we will speak of the Province of Quebec. When we discuss the independent state that may succeed the Province of Quebec, we will refer to the State of Quebec. Citizens of Canada resident in the Province of Quebec we will call Quebeckers. Citizens of the State of Quebec we will call Québécois.

When we speak of Canada without further qualification we mean the already existing state sans the Province of Quebec. In this respect we embrace the usage employed by the Quebec nationalists. When we intend to refer to Canada including the Province of Quebec we will say so. Usage regarding the State of Quebec vis-à-vis Canada will be unambiguous, since two sovereign countries will automatically be implied.

So much is clear and relatively straightforward. What follows is more contentious. Let us turn to the question: "What is liberal democracy?" So far as we are concerned, liberal democracy is based on four interrelated principles:

(1) Personal freedom. Citizens in liberal democracies are not coerced with respect to speech, religious liberty, private property, or the ability to oppose the government. Some liberal democrats favour government action to promote individual freedom and others think that any such government action dimin-

ishes freedom. Partisan disputes are inevitable, but both sides agree that personal freedom is a fundamental political good.

(2) Limited government. Liberal democrats believe that the state is charged with the primary task of preventing citizens from harming one another through force or fraud. The state defends the community and punishes lawbreakers. In addition it may promote the welfare of society in terms of specific economic, educational, and health policies; but under no circumstances does a liberal-democratic state attempt to take general charge of society.

(3) Equality of right or equality before the law. All citizens in a liberal democracy must abide by the same laws, which must be impartially administered by the state. There are neither "second-class" citizens nor aristocrats protected by their own special laws.

(4) Consent of the governed. Citizens in liberal democracies are aware that they are the source of government power and that the government is responsible to them. Accordingly, the people have the ability to change the government. Liberal democracy also implies that virtually all people are or can become citizens upon attaining the age of majority.

Liberal democrats can and do disagree about what constitutes social justice and what degree of government intervention in the economy, redistribution of wealth, or social equality is desirable, but they are in agreement that the majority must choose its own rulers, who in turn must govern within limits established by the law. The law provides for and safeguards equality of political rights.

By and large, liberal democracies are moderate political regimes, characterized by political bargaining and accommodation of divergent interests. Because this form of government is relatively mild, liberal-democratic societies tend to be prosperous. Because there are several ways of reconciling individual liberty and majority rule, a presidential as well as a parliamentary system of government is compatible with liberal-democratic principles. Canada, we believe, is quite clearly a liberal democracy. Moreover, as we shall explain in due course, a separate State of Quebec would also likely be a liberal democracy.

The current regime, which includes Quebec within Canada, poses a severe challenge to our liberal democracy, however, because of the political consequences of a complex of ethnically and culturally determined sentiments, aspirations, and demands that we have called Quebec nationalism. Many Quebeckers, virtually all the political leaders in the provincial government, and many MPs from that province share nationalist sentiments of this type. Quebec nationalism is a modern form of ethnic self-determination. It is similar to the various minority ethnic movements that sought self-determination within the Hapsburg Empire and achieved it, more or less, after the First World War. It is similar as well to the anticolonial movements that arose in the wake of the Second World War. The governing assumption of this type of nationalism holds that an ethnic group has a right to rule itself simply because it understands itself to be an ethnic group.

A second assumption of such nationalists, in Quebec or anyplace else, is that language is primarily a symbol of identity and only secondarily a means of communication. A Quebec nationalist will reply to the question, "Who are you?" with a response that emphasizes his or her identity as a Québécois. As a simple matter of fact, there exists a group of men and women currently in positions of political and intellectual leadership in the Province of Quebec who have activated in themselves and in others a collective self-identity based to a considerable extent on the French language. The founding document was the 1977 White Paper on Language, which declared at the outset that "the French in Quebec have never believed that their language could be dissociated from the destiny of the entire nationality, of its economy, and of its culture." This White Paper was a pure Quebec nationalist manifesto. The strongest thrust of Quebec's policy ever since has been to carry out the White Paper's implications. For reasons to be detailed in the course of this book, the Canadian government has alternately sought to accommodate or to appease the demands of the Quebec nationalists. In so doing, the Canadian government has carried water in a sieve. The national political agenda has been grossly distorted because, quite simply, Quebec nationalism does not conform to the usual and prudential politics of bargaining and mutual accommodation.

Third, Quebec nationalism is virtually an exclusive preserve of those men and women who see themselves as descendants of French colonists. Virtually anyone can learn to speak French and, with practice, some can even learn to speak accentless French. But not anyone can claim descent from French colonial forbears. And not all Quebeckers who can make such a claim endow this heritage with the symbolic significance that provides them with a collective identity. Those who do are the Quebec nationalists. For this reason we think it is accurate to speak of "the French" rather than francophone Quebeckers. So did the authors of the 1977 White Paper. By speaking of "the French," one captures the symbolic flavour of ethnic self-identification.

Despite certain similarities with European nationalism and third-world anticolonial movements, Quebec nationalism is distinct insofar as those who share its sentiments are resolutely modern. Quebec nationalism is not simply a phase in a centuries-long process of self-determination undertaken by an ethnic group. It is first of all a desire for individual self-determination within a modern technological society and state. Quebeckers who experience nationalist sentiments perceive the government of Canada and the current constitutional regime as an obstacle to their individual self-determination and the prospect of an independent Quebec as an aid to their own aspirations as modern men and women. For this reason they mobilize similar sentiments of ethnic identity in others and hold out the promise of both individual and collective self-determination as a goal.

The uneasy coexistence of individual and collective aspirations constitutes the fourth characteristic of Quebec nationalism. On the one hand, the French are men and women engaged in a quest for collective self-determination because they feel discriminated against, dominated by outsiders, frustrated by the existing federal political regime, and so on. On the other hand, however, they are, by and large, members of the new middle class created in the wake of the industrialization and secularization of French society. They are both the products and the beneficiaries of the replacement of the church by the provincial government in the areas of health, education, and welfare. They are fully conversant with the terms of the American dream. Like modern men and women everywhere in the world, Quebec's new middle class seeks the rewards of technological affluence: freedom, recognition, and the pleasurable satisfactions of personal achievement and fulfilled ambitions.

Whether collective and individual aspirations can be reconciled in a modern technological society has often been doubted. In Canada, George Grant has been the most eloquent critic of the attempt. Events, however, not theories, will constitute the final proof. For the present we merely note that the attitudes of the Quebec nationalists towards Canada are highly conditional. Since they and not, for example, the church, have custody of the French nation, and since the national purpose of the new middle class is miles away from the evangelical purposes of the church, the only question that matters to them is: Is Canada worth it? Does it pay the bills? Does the rest of Canada contribute enough towards the achievement of the aspirations of the French nation (aspirations that are, of course, indistinguishable from those of the new middle class), or does Canada inhibit those aspirations? The question of whether Canada is worthwhile in itself simply does not arise. It is for this reason that the new middle class is the heart and soul of Quebec nationalism, whether expressed by the BQ, the PQ, the Liberals, or the Conservatives.

Finally we would make the preliminary observation that Quebec nationalism requires a sense not only of "us" but also of "them." To the Quebec nationalist, to the French, the latter role is evoked by the term "English Canada." As we will see, however, nothing in the reality of Canadian political life corresponds to the term. Its meaning exists solely within the context of the Quebec nationalists' vision. This fact does not make for easy negotiations or even for honest acknowledgement of differences of opinion. As a practical matter this is another reason why Quebec must separate from Canada, and, for all our sakes, the sooner the better. In the course of this book, readers will find economic, historical, and political reasons why both countries, Canada and Quebec, will be better off as sovereign and independent states.

Not all Quebeckers share nationalist sentiments. There are, after all, those Westmount Rhodesians, as Keith Spicer once called the English-speaking, Anglo-Saxon Quebeckers; there are also non-French, non-Anglo-Saxon Quebeckers: Italians, Jews, Mohawks, Cree, Greeks, Chinese, Vietnamese, and so on. There are also a few old-style liberals, and Liberals who believe in dualism and federalism. For the moment, they are Quebeckers too. We are talking, however, about power in the Province of Quebec and about leadership. There is no question that a group of Quebeckers large enough and powerful enough seriously to impair the ability of the Canadian government to address the real problems of the country and to govern effectively has chosen the nationalist option. That is the reality that we ignore at our peril.

It is not our purpose to criticize or denounce ethnic and cultural nationalism, in Quebec or anywhere else. We wish to understand it and its political implications, particularly as they have an impact on Canada. The State of Quebec, we believe, would be capable of dealing with those same consequences when the time came to do so. In any event, and whether one approves of Quebec nationalism or not, it poses a grave problem to the existing constitutional order. Because of it, the real political agenda has been hijacked: Canada has too long diverted its energies towards a futile process of constitutional accommodation, ignoring its genuine economic, educational, industrial, and technological problems. The dream of constitutional accommodation was all dreamed out on June 23, 1990, when the Meech Lake Accord died. If the Meech Lake fiasco taught Canadians anything, it is that they cannot accommodate the demands of Quebec. As we will see in detail, this process is in no way mysterious or unintelligible: it is simply one consequence of recent political, social, and economic changes in Canada. Or rather, it is an intelligible response to those changes by Quebec's intellectual and political élite. We make no determinist arguments: things might have turned out differently. Quebec nationalism was by no means an inevitable response to the technological, social, and economic changes that Quebeckers have undergone. Nor was it the inevitable consequence of the inability of the Canadian Constitution to respond adequately to those changes or to changes elsewhere in the country. The point is: Quebec nationalism is the response that many Quebeckers have in fact made. And that fact has political consequences for everyone else. One of the aims of this book is to point some of them out.

Why do we believe that Quebec nationalism is incompatible with a Canadian liberal democracy that includes Quebec? To begin with, we sometimes forget that the attempt to solve the Quebec question has generated five different constitutions. Of these, the Proclamation of 1763 and the Act of Union of 1841 were clearly designed to forestall any problems associated with ethnic conflict by assimilating the French, lock, stock, and barrel. The other three constitutional arrangements, the Quebec Act (1774), the Constitutional Act (1791), and Confederation itself (1867), were in one way or another attempts at cohabitation or "dualism." The Constitution Act of 1982, by comparison, is neither fish nor fowl nor good red herring. It combines both centralizing and decentralizing principles, principles that acknowledge the importance of both individual and collective rights. None of these constitutions solved the Quebec problem. One of the reasons, we believe, is because none of them respected the principles of liberal-democratic constitutionalism. Instead, a pattern has developed where failed assimilation has given rise to dualism and then to nationalism of one kind or another. In the chapters that follow we will trace the shifts in the dominant climate of opinion in Quebec, from dualism and accommodation to nationalist withdrawal. We would recall, therefore, that separatism has always been an option. Common sense would suggest that, if the problem has not been solved by six constitutional experiments, all of which scrupulously avoided the obvious solution, then the time has come to try that obvious solution. But not only common sense suggests that Quebec must leave Canada. Reasons of principle also point in that direction.

Initially, constitutional government was established to enable people of different religious allegiances to live together. It did so by prohibiting the government from directly concerning itself with the salvation of the souls of its citizens. But in a secular age such as our own, questions of salvation are completely foreign to any government. Canada's experience from the Proclamation of 1763 to the present raises the question of whether, politically speaking, culture is equivalent to religion. This is meant to suggest not the blasphemous thought that culture is religious, but rather that, like religion in the seventeenth century, culture today may be an aspect of human life that should be banished from the public realm. Just as an established church is an anathema to a liberal constitutional democracy, so too is an established culture, nation, or ethnic group.

The analogy with religion can be pressed one step farther. The seventeenth- and eighteenth-century constitutionalists argued that it was possible to carry on political life without concern for the religious beliefs of one's fellow citizens. By the same reasoning, it ought to be possible to separate nation or culture and state. If there can be religiously neutral politics, there may be culturally neutral politics too. There may be. And, indeed, the relative longevity of our several dualist constitutional experiments indicates that there can be. In order to work, however, divergent religious or ethnic groups must agree that there should be a religiously or ethnically or culturally neutral sphere. And this the contemporary Quebec nationalist vehemently denies. Here is the core of the conflict of principles.

To put it another way, the soul of an ethnic and cultural nationalist is divided between liberal-democratic sentiments and illiberal premises or illiberal objectives. In contrast, the cultural pluralist is in this respect consistent with his or her liberal-democratic principles. As Rainer Knopff has pointed out, the illiberal elements in ethnic and cultural nationalism were as clear as could be in the response by the Parti Québécois to the results of the 1970 provincial election in Quebec. In that election, the PQ received 23 per cent of the popular vote but elected only 7 out of 110 members to the National Assembly. The "federalists" considered the 1970 election a clear statement of support for their policies. The PQ, however, declared that their miserable showing was a result of a rigged electoral system. The single-member constituency and the requirement that a plurality only is needed for election, the PQ said, exaggerated the power of cohesive minorities, namely the "English." Many PQ candidates, René Lévesque declared, had secured the majority of French votes but had been defeated by bloc voting by the non-French. In 1973 the PQ was again defeated decisively, and Lévesque issued a warning that the situation might become "explosive" if the English minority again kept in power a party not supported by the French majority.

On the surface this looks like a sustained support for majority rule. But in fact what counted for the PQ was not a majority of individual citizens but a majority of a majority ethnic group, the French. This is in profound disagreement with a cardinal assumption of liberal democracy, namely majority rule understood as the numerical majority of citizens. Liberals, remember, believe that citizens are equal. The Quebec nationalists argued, in effect, that they had a right to rule on behalf of the French not because the French were a majority but because they were French. They claimed this right because of the overriding importance of maintaining the Quebec nationalist political program. In short, what counts for Quebec nationalists are not the votes of citizens, but French votes.

The illiberal core of such a nationalism can be indicated in another way as well. The referendum on sovereignty-association in 1980 was held only in the Province of Quebec and not in Canada. Why? The answer, naturally enough, is that the reason for favouring sovereignty-association at all is essentially nationalistic, and the Province of Quebec is the only existing political unit that can serve as the basis for a homeland for the French of North America. It is the only political space where the French are a majority. By Quebec nationalist logic, the purpose of the government of Quebec, whether Quebec is a province of Canada or an independent state, is to represent the interests of the French and not the interests of the citizens of the Province of Quebec.

The implications, again, are illiberal. On the surface, the argument means that Quebeckers have the right to separate from Canada if their interests are ill served by the Canadian constitution. This seems fair enough. However, if it is the French as an ethnic or cultural group who enjoy the right to separate, then this right has nothing to do with their status as a majority in the Province of Quebec. The right being invoked is a right of self-determination and it exists whether or not the French are a majority or a minority.

The point can be underlined with a hypothetical case. If the French of North America were part of a unitary rather than a federal state like the Basques in Spain, would that accidental context make them relinquish their claims to independence? Of course not! The conclusion therefore is clear: the Quebec nationalist position is not intrinsically majoritarian or liberal-democratic. Characteristically, Quebec nationalist arguments appear to be based on democratic and majoritarian principles. But when push comes to shove, these principles are quickly abandoned: the overriding importance accorded to Quebec nationalist sentiments means that liberal, democratic, constitutional and majoritarian principles, however valuable they might be, are always secondary and incidental. But those principles, to a liberal democrat, are essential, not secondary.

We are now in a position to specify the "philosophical" reason why Canada cannot contain the nationalist fevers wracking the body politic of Quebec. Canada has been, is now, and ought to be in the future a liberal democracy. This means that the government must limit itself to the purpose of securing the rights of its citizens. The citizens themselves must exercise those rights as they see fit. This is what justifies majority rule. Moreover, it is what limits partisan disputes to the question of how best to secure the rights of citizens. In principle it excludes the right to rule on behalf of any particular way of life, or any particular ethnic group, culture, or religion. Since no particular group has a right to rule, not the French, not the Mohawks, not the Baptists or the Buddhists, not the intelligent or the left-handed, the only way to deal with partisan disagreements is by majority rule. And majorities do rule, not because they are right but because their rule is constituted by a majority of equal citizens.

Quebec nationalists will have none of this. They wish to rule because they are guardians of a particular way of life. That is why liberal democracy in Canada is in danger. As long as it is part of Canada, Quebec will be incapable of purging itself of French nationalist sentiments; therefore, both reason and prudence declare: Quebec must leave. The political implications of Quebec nationalism require separation.

A further point. In an independent Quebec, French nationalism would likely disappear. Francophones would be the overwhelming majority. "Challenges" from anglophones would be easily turned aside at the polling booths, and immigration to Quebec would probably be self-selecting — i.e., overwhelmingly francophone. For the first time since the conquest, francophone Quebeckers would have nothing to fear from anglophones and other minorities in their midst. There would be no need for special legislative protection for the French language or French culture. In other words, we believe that a State of Quebec would have no Bill 101, no Bill 178, no denial of anyone's right to express himself or herself in whatever language he or she chooses on the front of a store or anywhere else.

Having so strongly emphasized that we seek to understand a crisis and not to direct politicians and business leaders in the details of resolving it, we must reiterate that we are not so stupid, so disingenuous, or so naive as to think our analysis has no practical importance. We freely admit that we are liberal democrats and that we strongly support constitutional regimes. We, therefore, dispute the validity of ethnic and cultural nationalism as a sound foundation for decent government. And in any case, such nationalism has seldom served as a guide for the practice of government of any kind. But such implications and observations, however valid, are beside the point. It is both futile and condescending to argue that Quebec nationalists are wrong, that Canada is really their best hope, that they should be grateful for all Canada has done, that they are courting destruction by seeking to establish their own independent state. As a practical matter we believe Canada and a State of Quebec would both be better off, economically and politically, as two countries distinct in the same way as Spain is distinct from Norway. It is certainly our view that the current constitutional order works to the political advantage of neither Quebec nor Canada.

We have already indicated that the separation of Quebec from Canada is a first step to resolving the ongoing economic and constitutional crisis that we have endured for practically a generation. We will provide plenty of evidence to support these opinions. We will indicate what we see to be the consequences of separation both for the short term and for the long haul. Of course, we may be wrong in detail or simply wrong, period. Perhaps earlier visions of accommodation can be restored; perhaps Quebec nationalism will evaporate. We have every reason to doubt it. We freely admit we may be wrong about the consequences of separation, for no one can be certain about the future. But we are very confident that the Canadian state cannot remove itself from its chronic state of crisis so long as Quebec remains within it. *À nos amis en Québec nous disons: bon voyage et bonne chance!*

I

NAME YOUR CRISIS

Virtually every political event over the past couple of years in Canada has been tied to Quebec. One of the reasons Canada is currently in such an economic and political mess is that it has been unable to deal with the Quebec problem. Indeed, Canadians are almost embarrassed to talk about it as the Quebec problem. They prefer to use euphemisms and indirect speech, alluding to national unity or the restoration of the Canadian family or the completion of the constitutional process. But, however one describes the pattern of events, the consequences for the country are clear: without political support for the national government Canadians cannot muster the will to bite the bullet and tackle the real problems that beset them. Instead they have dithered interminably trying to square the constitutional circle. It cannot be done. The Quebec problem, the French-English problem, whatever you call it, cannot be solved. But because the Canadian public has been told by self-serving politicians and public servants that it can be, that it must be, that its solution is the overriding purpose of the nation, Canadians have lost faith in their leaders and in the constitutional order.

Why has this happened? It has happened because Canadians have been told for the past three decades that the solution to the Quebec problem is just around the corner. They have been told that one more compromise, one more series of negotiations, will do the trick. This is not unlike what the people of the United States were told during the Vietnam war — there is light at the end of the tunnel. They eventually discovered, to their horror, that the light at the end of the tunnel was the headlamp of an onrushing train.

Here then is the paradox. The problem is unsolvable, but Canada's government and political leaders have promised to solve it. They cannot solve it because it is unsolvable. Failure after failure destroys faith in government and trust in political leadership. The destruction of that faith and that trust leads to paralysis. Governments are now incapable of making the tough decisions that are necessary to solve all the other serious problems afflicting Canada today.

A short review of recent events underlines the obvious fact that we do have a Quebec problem and that our political leaders in Ottawa, in Quebec City, and in other provincial capitals have provided Canadians with a clear and distinct demonstration that they are incapable of handling it. Until Canadians wake up to this fact, they are wasting time, energy, and treasure in the pursuit of false visions and broken dreams. Until Canadians wake up to this fact, support for the government as a whole will continue to erode, and government will continue to be impotent in the face of tough economic issues. The vicious circle will continue.

Consider, then, the catalogue of recent events. On June 23, 1990, two days after summer officially began, the nation did not fall apart as Prime Minister Mulroney had promised it would if the Meech Lake Accord, supported by fully 25 per cent of all Canadians, was not ratified by the provincial legislatures. Brian Mulroney's great gamble failed, and he tumbled into a sulk for the rest of the summer. But we never would have entered the political swamp of Meech Lake had it not been for the demands of Quebec for special legal treatment. As might have been expected, the rest of the premiers objected to Quebec's being considered "more equal" under the law than the other provinces. Conceding special treatment to Quebec meant, in fact, granting areas of responsibility and power first to Quebec and then, for the most part, generalizing the concessions to the other provinces. Far from being evidence of political leadership — anyone, after all, can grant concessions — the Meech Lake fiasco was a clear indication of its absence. This is obvious from the aftermath as well.

After it had been denied legal authority for its claim to special status, Quebec saw an opportunity to take advantage of the new power vacuum. Provincially, Quebec announced the formation of a commission to develop constitutional alternatives. In Ottawa an ambitious and disgruntled MP from Quebec, Lucien Bouchard, left cabinet and government to found a groupscule of seven separatists, the Bloc Québécois. The leader of the Liberal Party, Jean Chrétien, remained beyond the gate; he eventually gained admittance to the House of Commons from nearby and complaisant New Brunswick and, with the assistance of his former colleagues, Pierre Trudeau and Don Johnson, he attempted to update an outdated vision of the place of Quebec in Canada. The major parties in Ottawa were clearly adrift and out of touch with events and with the sentiments that moved events.

Then the Mohawks went on the warpath in defence of some contested real estate and in protest against police attempts to curb their illegal activities along the Canada-U.S. border. The legal questions were complex, but the political one was simple. The Mohawks claimed to be a distinct society. They claimed not to be bound by the laws of Canada or Quebec in respect of excise tax or the importation of controlled substances. This was intolerable to Quebec, which also claimed to be a distinct society, and which called upon the army of Canada to deal with the native people. If one compares the way Ottawa and the Quebec government handled the Oka crisis with the way Ottawa and the government of British Columbia handled the Haida over the South Moresby Island crisis a year or so earlier, one thing seems clear: when dealing with Quebec, Ottawa appears to be incapable of giving direction to events but takes a back seat to local politicians. The rest of the country wonders why.

By autumn the Oka fever had spread across the country. Claiming autonomy, native leaders sought their own constitutional place in the sun, an additional special status to govern a scattered archipelago of reserves with a combined area about twice the size of Prince Edward Island.

Meanwhile the four western premiers were busy. They saw from the inside the attractions of special status and, like politicians everywhere, they wanted a piece of the pie. And so they invited Ottawa to get out of national social programs such as medicare and pensions. In exchange, the provincial governments would assume operating and tax responsibilities for these programs. Then they demanded a legislated ceiling on the expenditures of both the federal and the provincial governments. Third, they proposed an independent income-tax administration to set rates and collect revenue without overseeing from Ottawa. Lastly, they proposed provincial influence on national monetary policy, especially the interest rate. In Atlantic Canada, the premier of New Brunswick proposed joint external marketing programs and internal free trade for the region. Serious men and women in Alberta and British Columbia discussed a preferential trade area with the states of the Pacific Northwest, calling the new economic community "Cascadia." The significance of these and other similar proposals lies not in their workability as meaningful alternatives to current arrangements. The point is not whether a "Westbuck" would be stronger than the Canadian dollar. Rather, many Canadians have simply realized that the neighbourhood is falling apart and decided that all they can do is look after their own backyard.

And back in Ottawa, while Prime Minister Mulroney brooded at his summer residence, opposition mounted against the Goods and Services Tax, the centrepiece of his tax-reform program.

When fall arrived, opposition had become institutionalized in the unelected, unreformed, heretofore ineffective, and utterly unequal Senate. The democratically elected and, at least in theory, accountable and responsible House of Commons had passed legislation that 85 per cent of Canadians opposed. By a strange contingency, public opinion was reflected in the one institution established in such a way as to be insulated from public opinion.

Prime Minister Mulroney responded by accusing the Senate of being undemocratic. He forgot that it had been set up to be undemocratic, to provide "sober second thought" to misguided but popular legislation from the Commons. But in this instance the Senate represented the views of the overwhelming majority of Canadians. If anything, it was the House of Commons that was undemocratic. It was controlled by a single political party under strict discipline and with very low support in the nation. There may be many "sins" of which the Senate is guilty regarding the GST, but acting undemocratically isn't one of them.

Prime Minister Mulroney's response was unprecedented. Ever since he took office, he had opposed every serious attempt to make the Senate democratic and responsible; but now he went to the Queen for authority to appoint eight additional senators, each of whom would be as undemocratically elevated to the upper chamber as all their colleagues but one, Stan Waters of the Reform Party, and his appointment had been stalled for months.

As the fall wore on, Brian Mulroney confirmed his own dire predictions of the spring. Because Meech Lake failed, previously planned first ministers' meetings on the economy and on Senate reform would not take place. But in fact everyone knew there was no constitutional reason at all for cancelling the meeting on the economy. Ottawa simply wished to avoid public scrutiny and criticism of its policies. By elevating a routine political meeting into a constitutional impasse, Mulroney indicated that the country was ungovernable, that the machinery didn't work. Canadians, however, understood that it didn't work because Prime Minister Mulroney had ensured it wouldn't work.

In the case of Senate reform, the premiers, with or without the prime minister and with or without a representative from Quebec, can meet to discuss any matter they wish. Holding or not holding a conference has nothing to do with Meech Lake. We know that the failure of Meech Lake has not prevented bilateral constitutional discussions between Ottawa and Quebec. It is troubling to Canadians outside Ottawa that they have no place at the table. It is troubling to Canadians outside Quebec that Prime Minister Mulroney seems to be punishing the rest of the country for ignoring the demands of his home province. The implication is ominous indeed: when Quebec decides to stay home, as with Senate reform, it is not a "national" issue. But the rest of the country can be excluded when Quebec's interests are involved, as with control over immigration.

The immigration agreement concluded between Ottawa and Quebec City in January 1991 is particularly vexing because it is virtually identical to one of the provisions of the now-defunct Meech Lake Accord. Quebec has stated its wish to obtain a quarter of all immigrants, which is in line with its share of Canada's population. In addition, however, it is seeking an additional 5 per cent to compensate for its low birth rate. At the same time as Quebec is demanding more immigrants to compensate for demographic deficiencies, we learn that the *bébé-bonus* inaugurated by the Quebec government is having the hoped-for effect. In 1990, for instance, the number of babies born in Quebec increased by 6 per cent. Of course, it will take some time to reach demographic stability, but it is by no means self-evident that Canadians have an interest in paying for population-management programs and problems in a nationalist Quebec. In fact, however, Canadian taxpayers are paying the government of Quebec $332 million to take over what had been the responsibilities of Ottawa. Would such a policy even be considered, let alone justified in terms of the national interest, if it were applied to Manitoba or Newfoundland, where the decline in population has been proportionately much larger? The argument seems to be that, so far as the rest of Canada is concerned, market forces can decide the destination of immigrants. But when immigrants don't make the right choice (and clearly they have not, since Quebec has received only about 16 per cent of immigrants over the past few years), then the government of Canada must step in and sweeten the pot. Since the agreement between Quebec and Canada still respects the right of immigrants to leave Quebec for other provinces, one wonders what further restrictions may be contemplated if immigrants choose to exercise their mobility rights. In any event, the pattern of giving something first to Quebec and then to the other provinces has been followed in the new immigration policy. Soon after Quebec got what it wanted, Ontario presented its demands.

Generally speaking, the aftermath of Meech Lake has consisted of concessions, bungling, and petulance. The Canadian ship of state seems to have no one at the helm. It is no wonder that Canadians have lost confidence not simply in the government of the day or the leaders of any particular party, but in the whole way they have been ruled. The context for much of this discontent, of course, is the economy and the persistent mismanagement of it by a generation of political leaders. But one must be wilfully blind not to see that the economy and the Quebec problem are connected. We believe one of the major reasons the government of Canada has done such a bad job managing the economy is because it has had to devote so much energy, talent, and, yes, money to the Quebec problem. The problem has not gone away and it has not been dealt with effectively. It has grown larger and the solution seems even more remote. Quebec is discontented with the rest of Canada, and the rest of Canada is fed up with Quebec. These are not happy times.

Profile of Discontent

In recent years, Canadians have had to come to terms with a bewildering array of poorly conceived constitutional changes and misguided constitutional practices. One of the most interesting constitutional proposals has, unfortunately, never been considered. It would stipulate that, when the percentage of the population supporting the government drops below the prime lending rate, the governor general would be obliged to call an election. This proposal, fanciful though it may seem, indicates clearly the interconnection between bad policy, especially bad economic policy, and support, or rather lack of support, for the government.

There is plenty of evidence that the two are connected. During the recession of the early 1980s, twice as many Canadians expected things to get worse as expected them to get better. We have only recently begun to think that way again. Since 1983, for the biblical allotment of seven fat years, Canadians have looked forward to each new year with confidence, not concern. According to any number of Gallup polls, we have been one of the most optimistic peoples in the world. By 1990 our optimism had evaporated. Canadians now seem to be bracing themselves for seven lean years.

Our confidence in political parties — all political parties — is low. Fewer than a third of us have much respect for the House of Commons. On the other side of the ledger, early in 1990 more than seven Canadians in ten believed the country to be on the wrong political and economic course, an increase of nearly 20 per cent from 1989. Outside Quebec, public support for federal authorities is at an all-time low. In September 1990, only 17 per cent of all Canadians had much confidence in Ottawa. Support for the provincial governments was higher, but only in Quebec were provincial authorities even moderately respected.

When one looks at support for the Conservative Party, the decline from 1988, to say nothing of 1984, is breath-taking. As late as January 1989, the Mulroney government was supported by half the Canadian electorate (and nearly two-thirds of Quebeckers). Ten months later its support across the country had been halved, though attrition in Quebec was comparatively minor. During the spring of 1990 the Conservatives made polling history. In April only 16 per cent of Canadians favoured the Tories, the lowest rating for a government party in fifty years of poll-taking. Even during the long period of Liberal ascendancy during the 1940s and 1950s when they toiled under the uninspiring leadership of John Bracken and George Drew, the Conservatives did better than that. By the end of the summer, after the failure of Meech Lake and the election of Jean Chrétien as leader of the Liberal Party, the Tory stock had risen only in Quebec.

The approval-rating of Brian Mulroney followed closely the decline in support for his party. In July 1990, for example, only 14 per cent of Canadians thought he was doing a good job. Only in Quebec, it seems, did Mulroney emerge as the citizens' choice for prime minister. One inspired poll conducted during the spring of 1990 asked Canadians to compare Brian Mulroney and Pierre Trudeau. A year earlier, nearly a quarter more Canadians preferred Mulroney; this time Trudeau won hands down.

It is true that some of this disdain for the Conservatives is simply a reflection of normal fluctuations in popular support for the government. Between elections, large numbers of voters often park themselves in the ranks of the undecided. Some of these people are not very interested in politics anyhow: it takes the noise and ballyhoo of an election simply to get their attention. A few are genuinely independent and have prudently decided to reserve judgement until election time. Many more electors, however, express their discontent with the government or the economy, their sense that their expectations are endangered and their hopes for improvement thwarted, by criticizing the government and the prime minister, no matter who they are. Even with all these qualifications, however, two things seem obvious. First, support for the government of Brian Mulroney is astonishingly low right across the nation. Second, Quebec is significantly out of step. Comparatively speaking, Quebeckers seem less discontented with the Tories than the rest of Canadians, and express greater approval of Prime Minister Mulroney.

Even more than fluctuations in public opinion, elections provide a focus for discontent. Politicians often think people vote for them and for the enlightened policies they have promised to enact or support; in fact, people are as likely to have voted against losers as for the winners. It is a long-standing political myth that elections resolve policy differences. Once the smoke of the electoral battle clears, it is said, the victorious government declares itself to have achieved a mandate to implement its policies. In fact, this hardly ever happens. In 1988 the single-issue "Free Trade Election" was the great exception in recent years. Most of the time elections are fought over such vague and general issues as the economy or unemployment or inflation.

On occasion, "leadership" is an issue. Who can forget the dramatic accusation of Brian Mulroney, finger pointed in mock outrage at John Turner? "You had an option, sir!" he thundered in August 1984, when Turner declared he had been obliged to appoint a bevy of Liberal Party hacks to the Senate and to other patronage positions. A few years later, Brian Mulroney "had to" appoint, in the space of a few weeks, twenty-three new senators. No doubt Prime Minister Mulroney can come up with his own distinct reasons or excuses, but his action was identical with that of his Liberal predecessor. There was, in fact, no change in policy. When journalists noticed that Canadians saw little difference between Liberals and Conservatives, they discovered a leadership crisis.

Almost everyone agrees that leadership is an important political commodity, even in a democracy. Sometimes greatness is thrust upon the people who happen to hold office during critical times; sometimes we get the leaders we deserve. The alchemy of individual and opportunity is mysterious, and not all leaders rise to the occasion. In 1932, one of the few great statesmen of this century, Winston Churchill, put it this way: "Is the march of events ordered and guided by eminent men; or do our leaders merely fall into their places at the heads of the moving columns?" Real leadership, he said, demands that prudent men and women order events. Those who find themselves at the heads of moving columns are simply managers of opinion; in modern political life they are career demagogues guided by the latest polls. It may be that Prime Minister Mulroney and the provincial premiers consider themselves to be "eminent men" in Churchill's sense. It may be that they rejoice in having record low levels of popular support. Perhaps they think that the absence of approval means they are not cut-out characters at the heads of moving columns. Unfortunately, the evidence is against them.

To take only the examples familiar from the summer of 1990 in Quebec: for several months before the Sûreté du Québec stormed the Mohawk barricades at Oka and was so ignominiously repulsed, the revolt or rebellion was allowed to simmer. In other words, criminal behaviour was tolerated. For more than a year proposals had been suggested to establish a royal commission to look into the condition of aboriginal peoples. In June 1990, Prime Minister Mulroney allowed that it was an idea whose time had come. All he was asking in return was that the native peoples of Manitoba support the Meech Lake Accord. When they rejected his offer, he withdrew it completely and added that he never really thought much of the idea anyway. In other words, the offer of a royal commission was a negotiating ploy, not evidence of serious concern for the political and economic place of native people in Canada. One need not be a native Canadian with a direct interest in having the government look into a serious problem in order to view Mulroney's moves as transparently cynical and dishonest. At a time when mere honesty is the first thing voters list as desirable in a political leader, such actions are even more to be deplored.

Even after the Oka crisis had demonstrated the pusillanimity of the leaders of Canada and of Quebec, it was emphasized again by the blockade of the Mercier Bridge and the riots by the inconvenienced residents of the South Shore. The voters of the Montreal riding of Laurier-Sainte-Marie sent the same message to Ottawa when they voted for a candidate who proposed to dismantle the parliamentary institution to which he had been elected. Clearly these electors did not find effective leadership in the government, headed by a Quebecker, that they had helped elect a few years earlier. Nor could they support the Liberal Party, even though they had done so in Laurier-Sainte-Marie in the 1988 election. Indeed, the leader of the Liberal Party, the once and perhaps future "little guy from Shawinigan," was widely believed to be unelectable in his home province. Moreover, Jean Chrétien's answer to the Oka mess was just as unsavoury as Prime Minister Mulroney's: Chrétien proposed to let the Mohawks go and arrest them later. The message was clear: when Quebec intrudes into areas of Ottawa's primary jurisdiction, such as native affairs, Ottawa will sacrifice its responsibilities for fear of offending Quebeckers. And when Quebec proves that it is as incompetent as Ottawa, as it surely did at Oka and Khanesatake, Ottawa steps in without complaint and without criticism to pull the province's chestnuts from the fire.

A comical example of the current connection between public cynicism and lack of leadership came from the 1990 Ontario provincial election. The leader of the Ontario Conservatives, Michael Harris, observed: "Unless we can restore confidence in our government, I fear government itself will deteriorate." The same issue of the *Globe and Mail* that reported his statement (September 5, 1990) carried a story indicating as clearly as possible that Harris had things exactly backwards. The headline read: "75 MPs reach pension milestone." The story began by noting that September 4, 1990, marked the day when seventy-five members of Parliament, first elected when Brian Mulroney came to power in 1984, became eligible for their pensions. None resigned in order to cash in, but Canadians were none the less surprised and angry to learn that the cost to the taxpayer — themselves — if the MPs in fact had quit was $30 million. The truth was the exact opposite of Michael Harris's statement: government has deteriorated and that is why so many Canadians have no confidence in it.

The evidence from the polls and from the media indicates that we do not trust our leaders. Over the past two decades, the real and pressing problems of the economy and of the constitutional order have not been resolved by the prudent actions of statesmen. Instead of seeing economic and political discontent for what they are — manifestations of deep-seated problems — politicians have preferred to treat them as narrow, short-term grievances, addressing them not with vision and fundamental changes or long-term strategies, but with quick-fix expedients. Accordingly, elections have not delivered mandates to governments, and governments have not responded to continuing problems or to what might be termed structural flaws. Instead, they have viewed problems as simple dislocations that could be fixed up by a new policy initiative, or fresh leadership, or perhaps a task force or royal commission if things looked at all serious.

Even in politics, the chickens come home to roost. We can see this stubborn and unavoidable truth most dramatically in the disintegration of the Soviet empire in Eastern and Central Europe: at long last the real and avoidable inefficiencies of tyranny have overtaken the fantasies of ideology, and the whole structure has crumbled. A similar but less bloody process is unfolding in our own country. As in the Soviet Union, the structural inefficiencies of Canada are also chiefly economic and are tied to the consequences of excessive administration. In short, the context for understanding our current political malaise, so faithfully reflected in public-opinion polls, is to look at the financial mess the country is in. We are not saying that Quebec has caused our debt crisis, though it has in fact done more than its fair share. We are saying that, without the insoluble Quebec question, our political leaders would have an opportunity to focus their undoubted talents more clearly on the real problems of Canada.

We are saying as well that the nationalist aspirations of Quebeckers are of concern to them and to them alone. In this respect, as well, Canada's problems are similar to the Soviet ones: Canadians' fantasies and dreams are political. These fantasies, unlike the Soviet ones, have nothing to do with the ideological nonsense of Marxism. Instead, we have created a chronic constitutional crisis at the centre of which is the incompatibility of Quebec's nationalist aspirations with Canadian liberal democracy.

To use parliamentary language, it is time to put the question: Is Quebec in or out of Canada? We cannot continue with what the late Eugene Forsey called hemi-, demi-, semi-separatism, with separatism as a threat, but not an objective. The problem is not in the Quebec question itself but in the refusal of politicians in positions of responsibility to answer it. Hence, we believe, the low esteem in which our leaders are held. Hence the low support for the entire constitutional order. Hence the malaise and discontent, the sense of foreboding that is reflected in our public-opinion polls.

Hence, too, an important reason for our spiralling debt. When our political leaders are unwilling to confront the major political issue of the day, the Quebec question, why should we expect them to confront the major economic issue, the debt? After all, the same pusillanimous, waffling, double-talking individuals are involved. To use the language of Robert Borden, prime minister from 1911 to 1920, what they want is spine and backbone. And if they lack the requisite talent or backbone to deal with the Quebec question, we should not be surprised when they prove incapable of dealing with the economy. The convergence of these two problems provides Canadian political leaders with a reality they can no longer avoid. It also provides them with an opportunity to deal with them both in a tolerably adequate way. In due course we will indicate how. First, however, let us examine the economic crisis.

The Debt and How to Make It Grow

The second prime minister of Canada, Alexander Mackenzie, had both the virtues and the flamboyance of a bookkeeper. Historians are uniform in their agreement that he was not a man of vision but one of caution. Perhaps the time has come again for the dull virtues of fiscal prudence. Let us consider recent budgetary history.

The purpose of the expenditure budget is to indicate in dollars and cents who gets what from the government. It signals to the world, which includes both the civil service and ordinary Canadians, what the government thinks is important. Just as game is always scarce for the hunter, so too are revenues always in short supply, especially for new programs. The expenditure budget, therefore, is a way of keeping score. By noticing who gets what, one has a good idea of who the winners and losers are. A glance at the budgets of the past generation indicates that there have been many more winners than losers.

It is common knowledge that government spending has grossly increased. The numbers involved are impressive. In 1939 the total budgetary expenditure was around $550 million; in 1950 it was $2.4 billion (2,400 million); by 1960 it had reached $6.7 billion; by 1970, $15.3 billion; by 1980, $62 billion; and by 1990, $143 billion. When one looks at expenditures as a percentage of gross domestic product or GDP, one finds the same pattern of increase. This measure is a more accurate indication of the growth in government spending and intrusiveness because it takes into account the absolute growth in the size of the economy. In 1940, during wartime, the federal expenditure budget was about 16 per cent of GDP; by 1950 it had fallen to below 13 per cent; in both 1960 and 1970 it was nearly 18 per cent; by 1980 it had reached 20 per cent and by 1990, 22 per cent. At the same time the net public debt had increased from a relatively modest $18 billion in 1970 to $86 billion in 1980; as we write it is approaching $400 billion. A final indication of the nation's financial health is to consider how much of the budget is allocated to paying interest on the national debt. As with personal credit cards, money spent on debt servicing comes off the top. The finance minister himself said in the 1990 budget speech: it "is money we can't use now to get taxes down or to address priorities such as environmental protection, research and development and skills training. We must pay those interest costs." In 1960 those interest costs amounted to about 11 per cent of budget expenditures; in 1970, around 12 per cent. By 1980 more than 16 per cent of the budget expenditure was devoted to debt servicing, and in 1990 the figure stands at close to 40 per cent. To make matters worse, these startling results were achieved during a period of significant economic expansion. When the economy contracts, as it appears to be doing at present, the problem will get worse because demands on the social-welfare system will increase.

Other equally disheartening statistics could be introduced to indicate Canada's massive financial overextension. Canadians, like most human beings, can distinguish between people who pay their bills and people who don't. We know we are in deep trouble as a nation when the government is more concerned with its ability to borrow than it is with its ability to pay. More to the point, foreign lenders are fully aware that our current high standard of living has been sustained by offshore borrowing. One need not be initiated into the arcane world of international finance to realize that our foreign exposure is not reassuring either to ourselves or to our creditors.

In response to failed and misguided industrial initiatives such as the National Energy Program, the Foreign Investment Review Agency (FIRA), and the Scientific Research Tax Credit, the Conservatives have tried to reverse field. Looking back on the failures, the government and the bureaucrats are agreed that they are ill equipped to pick winners and to encourage "sunrise" industries. Many have come to the correct conclusion that experimenting with Crown corporations in so-called key sectors of the economy has simply produced inefficient and bloated organizations capable of consuming enormous sums of money. To no one's surprise, a disproportionate amount of this chunky-style pork-barrelling has gone to inefficient and obsolete industries in Quebec.

Even though the Conservatives could see the problems, they seem incapable of solving them. Their macro-economic policy, for instance, is based on gross but relatively simple errors, obvious to everyone but themselves. In the early years following the Free Trade Agreement with the United States, Canada needs a low dollar to help Canadians penetrate the American market. We have a high one. In order to cushion our adjustment to free trade, we need a strong economy. We have the lowest growth rate since the last recession. In order to improve Canadian competitiveness, we need low interest rates. Interest rates have remained unconscionably high, especially in light of the importance of resource exports in Canada's economy.

We have either no industrial strategy at all or one so badly distorted by politics as to be useless. Canadian research and development is a joke; the consequence is that Canadian workers (and those in Quebec as well) are unprepared for the technologies of the 'nineties. Computers and biotechnology have their rightful place in the economy, but not at the expense of our traditional strengths in industrial manufacturing and resource extraction. How much has been done to encourage Canadian manufacturers to respond to major changes in materials technologies? When the plastics industry spends millions of dollars each year to develop substitutes for metals, the hard-rock miners of Canada and the Canadian mining companies are involved, whether they like it or not. In the area of resources generally, Canadian companies have concentrated their efforts on improving extraction processes, not on developing new products and not on downstream processing.

The government has pursued a high-tech agenda only in the fields of space technology and biotechnology. And there its institutional support has been massively and disproportionately located in Quebec. These and other projects foisted onto Canadians in the name of regional development are simply political tools. The only beneficiaries of the high-tech initiatives, for example, have been the privileged residents living in the fantasyland of "Silicon Valley North," a notional location in the Ottawa-Hull-Montreal area. In no sense do these government actions constitute a rational economic policy. Consequently, there should be no expectation that they will result in rational economic development.

The government's response, of course, is that so long as the debt is so high they cannot pursue a rational policy. We agree. Under the circumstances, then, the government is faced with a simple choice: either lower expenditures or raise revenues. According to a Gallup poll released in April 1989, the Canadian public strongly supported reductions in expenditures. Universality in social programs was not sacrosanct; unemployment insurance could be cut, along with defence spending. According to Gallup, the data suggested "that the government would be best advised to concentrate on spending cuts rather than tax increases as a method to reduce the deficit. Fully ninety percent of Canadians prefer expenditure reduction rather than tax hikes as a deficit-reducing approach." In addition, Canadians have long been convinced that the government is wasteful and that MPs are paid too much. And finally, with the significant exception of Quebec, a clear majority of Canadians consider "big government" more of a threat to the future of the country than either big business or big labour unions.

Political leaders know this. In the past twenty years, four governments, two Liberal and two Conservative, have solemnly declared the number-one priority to be fiscal restraint, fair taxes, and regional economic balance. In his first budget in 1984 Michael Wilson declared that the highest priority would be given to setting Canada's fiscal house in order. In his 1990 budget he claimed great success in having stuck to his guns. Most Canadians didn't believe him. Shortly after the budget came down, Canadians were polled for their views regarding its significance. Fully seven out of ten Canadians did not agree with the view that the budget would strengthen the economy. This degree of dissent established another Gallup record. A few months later, when the implications of a higher deficit and new taxes had sunk in, only 16 per cent of Canadians thought the Tories were handling the economy properly. In Quebec support for the government's economic policy was significantly higher, at 25 per cent.

Leaving Quebec aside for a moment, we are faced with a very curious picture. First, everyone knows that a series of large deficits has resulted in an enormous debt, the servicing of which is costing all Canadians a lot of money each year. Debt servicing also means that the government is severely restricted in its ability to initiate new programs — environmental protection, research and development, and skills training, to repeat Michael Wilson's quite reasonable list of desiderata. An entire generation of politically aware finance ministers has declared that the debt was an enormous problem, that they were about to fix it, and that they would do so by reducing expenditures. Nothing has happened. Instead we are now faced with a higher debt, higher debt-servicing charges, and new taxes. Instead of cutting expenses it looks as though the government is again trying to raise revenue. Which brings us to the Goods and Services Tax — the GST. The one thing the GST has done is to add to the general crisis of confidence in the government. Why?

The GST is the second phase of a tax-reform initiative launched in June 1987, with the release of a White Paper on tax reform. The first phase dealt with income tax and came into effect in 1988 with comparatively little opposition. Nearly everyone who has examined the Canadian tax system agreed that the federal Manufacturers' Sales Tax, the MST, had to be replaced. It was based on a narrow range of goods and was applied at an early stage in the manufacturing process. As a result, it became embedded in the basic price of manufactured goods, so that secondary producers ended up paying tax on tax. In addition, it was applied at a highly variable rate. For these reasons Michael Wilson called the MST a "silent killer of jobs." And, indeed, most tax experts agreed that the MST did distort investment decisions and that, generally speaking, it had a negative impact on the efficiency of the economy.

The GST was intended to be more efficient than the MST, and nearly everyone agrees that, in this respect, it is a marked improvement. Moreover, conventional wisdom suggests that the GST is less regressive than the MST because it is spread over a larger range of commodities in such a way that it has a greater impact on higher-income households. On the other hand, the

GST was designed to increase revenues, and not simply to replace revenue lost with the expiry of the MST. As a result, a larger share of federal revenue will come from this tax than from income taxes. The GST is certainly more regressive than the income tax and, broadly speaking, it looks to be a regressive tax. However, most tax analysts agree that the impact of the GST remains unclear, even when the enriched refundable tax credits for low-income families are factored in. Other uncertainties surround the long- and short-term impact on growth, investment, income, inflation, interest rates, and administrative costs.

In two important areas, however, there are no uncertainties. The pledge contained in the 1987 White Paper that the GST would raise no more revenue than the old system, that it would be "revenue neutral," has clearly been scrapped. Second, the GST is highly visible. These two features of the GST politically reinforce each other, a fact that has helped increase opposition to the government and contributed to the general climate of crisis.

There are several reasons why the government has run into so much trouble over the GST. First, the replacement of an invisible tax, no matter how inefficient, with a visible one is bound to be politically costly. For many taxpayers, a newly visible replacement tax looks like a new tax pure and simple. And what looks like a new tax can be identified easily enough as another taxgrab. Most of us are concerned with how much tax we have to pay right now and not with diffuse benefits to the economy as a whole that will effect us only indirectly and over the long term. When the new tax is seen to be revenue enhancing, this simply makes matters worse: taxpayers lose and the government wins. Finally, the government was inept in its timing of the GST. As long ago as the Carter Royal Commission on Taxation in 1966, tax reform along the lines of the GST had been proposed. It is not clear why the Mulroney government decided to revive this proposal in its 1987 White Paper, though plausible economic reasons, such as the increasing inefficiency of the MST, could be cited. But it was a major blunder to introduce an obviously unpopular tax policy in the sixth year in office, after having already raised taxes several times. You do not have to be particularly Machiavellian to realize that the time to introduce tax reform is in the early years, when a government still has some political capital to spend.

Technically speaking, the GST is not a particularly odious tax. In a democracy, invisible taxes such as the MST are not a good thing. They hide government responsibility and diminish accountability. One can even make a case for increasing revenue in order to reduce the deficit and lower the national debt. In short, the widespread and vehement opposition to the GST is evidence of the lack of prudence of the government, a response to its generally low level of leadership qualities — a reaction not based on economic considerations alone.

The admission by the minister of finance that the GST would not be revenue neutral but would, in fact, be revenue enhancing and that the additional revenue would be used to reduce the debt raises again the curious question: Why have so many governments found it impossible to cut expenditures? The answer usually offered by politicians — that the Canadian electorate looks to the government to do things and to give them gifts and never to take anything away — is contradicted by public-opinion surveys that indicate persistent support for cutting allegedly sacred programs and reducing the size of government. If leaner does indeed mean meaner, then Canadians seem to be ready to accept a meaner government. One thing, in any event, is very clear: we will never know if reduced government services are acceptable until it is tried. And it has never ever been tried. Why not?

The short answer is: because the government is incapable of managing the public sector. To see why this is so we have to look more closely at the politics and administration of public spending in Canada. During the 1930s several of the young men who, after the Second World War, became high-ranking Canadian civil-service mandarins sat at the feet of the economist John Maynard Keynes, or otherwise encountered his views and accepted them as true. Keynes had argued that the government was capable of managing the economy in such a way that the cycle of boom and bust could be replaced by economic swings of a much smaller amplitude. The chief means of so doing was by adjusting taxation rates in a progressive direction and by using the spending and purchasing power of the government to "stimulate" falling demand, not least of all by creating generous social-welfare policies. In times of economic contraction and lowered revenues, the theory went, the government should run a deficit rather than cut services and try to maintain a balanced budget on an annual basis. When the economy picked up again, increased revenues from taxation could be applied to the accumulated annual deficits. In this way, over the long term, the debt would be reduced to zero and the budget would be balanced.

During the 1930s the apprentice Keynesians in Ottawa were appalled at the economic disaster of the Depression; during the war they were equally appalled at the cost of economic rejuvenation. As the war drew to a close they feared that the productive machinery that had sustained the war effort would break down and the nation would again be mired in an economic depression. After the First World War there had been strikes and riots; they feared that the economic dislocation would be worse this time because the economy was so much larger and more complex. Moreover, the political, economic, and ideological problems thrown up by the Depression had only been masked by the war, not dealt with. Only a few people, most notably the ever-ebullient C.D. Howe, insisted that the war had produced new economic opportunities in communications, in electronics, and, above all, in automobile manufacturing. Most political leaders and most government economists expected a grave economic downturn if the market were allowed to operate without government influence. Here was Keynes's great appeal. His economic doctrines promised a smooth transition to prosperity. The government should put money into the hands of those who needed it and who would spend it. Ordinary Canadians would be directly helped, and indirectly the expansive economy would ensure the maintenance of a high level of employment. By this argument, deficit financing would stabilize the entire economy, and the social-welfare legislation it supported would improve the condition of those in need.

The doctrine proved irresistible. To the mandarins it promised both real power and the even greater satisfactions that come from the knowledge of doing the right thing in the national interest. To the political leaders in the Liberal Party, it seemed a way to avoid the anticipated post-war depression and sustain themselves in office. As well, Keynes's technical approach to economic management bypassed the political and ideologically charged debates of the 1930s when "the capitalist system" as a whole was called into question. Both government politicians and government bureaucrats sought to reconstruct capitalism and liberal democracy, not destroy it. Accordingly, as the war was drawing to an end, they appointed an arch-mandarin, W.A. Mackintosh, to chair the Economic Advisory Committee and plan for post-war economic reconstruction. Keynes had indicated the measures needed. They were outlined in the April 1945 White Paper on Employment and Income and in the Green Book proposals for the Dominion-Provincial Conference on Reconstruction later the same year.

In order to plan at all, however, to say nothing of undertaking to implement Keynesian "counter-cyclical" economic doctrines, planners and administrators needed information. The economy had to be monitored before it could be managed. This meant that government would have to grow. Or rather, it meant that it would not shrink as much as it would have done after the war in the absence of Keynesian doctrines. In addition, the greatest amount of non-shrinkage would invariably be in Ottawa, not the provincial capitals, at least at the beginning of the Keynesian era.

Some critics have questioned whether government policy in the post-war world was really Keynesian or merely used Keynesian terminology to justify an increased government presence in the economic affairs of the nation. The Conservative leader of the opposition, George Drew, went so far as to accuse C.D.

Howe, of all people, of being a closet Marxist because of the extent to which he advocated government intervention in the economy. This was surely rhetorical overkill; but it did draw attention to the fact that the greatest defect in Keynes's theory lay not in the area of economics at all, but in its political implications. In a time of economic contraction, governments acting on Keynesian principles have not found it terribly difficult to increase government spending. But it is much more difficult to restrain expenditures during periods of economic expansion. After all, with more money coming in there is an opportunity to introduce new policies without cutting back on old ones. When times are tough you can increase the debt on good Keynesian grounds; and when things get better, there is even more money to spend. The latter is not what Keynes had in mind, but he was merely an economist, not a politician or a public servant.

This pattern of spending, which we might call perverse Keynesianism, has been in place for well over a generation. Other apparently unavoidable factors have also encouraged government growth. New kinds of economic activity, mega-projects, rising per-capita income, urbanization, technological integration of geographically dispersed activities, and environmental and social-welfare policies have all sustained the demand for services that the government was said to be best suited to deliver. An aging population promises to increase the strain on health care and pension resources. Governments are convinced that cutting back on anything carries a political cost that is best avoided. In this they are right, at least for the short term. And, as British prime minister Harold Wilson once said, "in politics, a week is a long time." The difficulty with this way of operating is that real problems don't often go away on their own. Usually a refusal to spend political capital today leads to a bigger bill tomorrow.

In a federal system like ours, pressures for increased expenditures come not only from individual citizens and pressure groups but also from provincial governments. And when provincial governments are the sources of new demands, the strain on budgetary rectitude grows astronomically. From regional economic development to control over immigration, a major source of new provincial demands has been Quebec. We will discuss the reasons for this later. The point to be made here is that whatever is given to Quebec must usually be balanced by similar conces- sions to all the other provinces. In short, we have a fiscal ratchet: the debt always goes up and never comes down.

There probably was very little that could have been done to avoid a certain amount of growth in government in the post-war era. Since 1970 or so, however, a series of highly avoidable mea- sures have been undertaken that have made it easier to make the debt grow in the name of managing the economy. To see how this worked we have to take a closer look at how the federal government is organized.

Why Spenders Win

A common way to distinguish government departments is to see whether the purpose of a department is chiefly to spend money or to control spending. In Canada the "guardians" are the Department of Finance and Treasury Board. The spenders are everyone else. The task of a spending minister, very simply, is to get as much as possible from Finance, even though ministers know it is better not to run a deficit and even though they know it is government policy to reduce the debt.

The dynamics of the problem are not hard to understand. Assume you are a cabinet minister. You know it is in the interest of the cabinet as a whole to reduce expenditures, which is why it is government policy in the first place. But you also know it is not in your own interest as a cabinet minister to reduce your own particular budget. You know that your own programs, after all, are necessary, just, and in the public interest. You know that you are an efficient administrator. If there are to be cuts, you know they should come from other departments where there is fat to be trimmed. When all cabinet ministers think this way (and they usually all do), there are four possible outcomes. The worst possible outcome would be for your own budget to be reduced and the surplus to go to another ministry, which would surely waste it. The best possible outcome would be to have all ministers reduce their budgetary expenditures but you. But since your colleagues think the same way about you as you do about them, no one has any reason to trust anyone else or any reason to co-operate. So there is no way to reduce everyone's budget. What is acceptable to you is to ensure that your budget isn't cut; and if that means that no one else's budget is cut either, well, you can live with that. No one around the cabinet table loses, and the taxpayer picks up the tab.

The problem can also be explained as a variation on the attraction of a free lunch. If you go to lunch with several other people you can either go Dutch and ask the waiter for separate cheques, or you can ask for one cheque and split it equally. If you are paying for it yourself, a hamburger and a beer look pretty good. If you ask for one cheque, it is in your immediate interest to order a couple of martinis, a steak sandwich, a saucy Beaujolais, and a couple of shooters afterwards, on the theory that the rest of the group will share the extra cost. If everybody thinks that way and you pay on one cheque, the bill is a lot higher than it would be if everyone paid separately. Formally, this situation is known as "prisoner's dilemma." We will see that it applies to the bureaucracy as well as to elected officials sitting around the cabinet table.

Transferring the example to government, it seems that ministers and bureaucrats always insist on one cheque, and it is up to the finance minister to see to it that they all order burgers and beer. He knows full well that if he agrees to allow one minister to increase expenditures (order a steak sandwich) on political grounds, he will be besieged with requests from others with equally valid spending proposals. As one observer said, the minister of finance is like a goalie in hockey: he is good at stopping things, but he can't score. Even so, a good goalie can often decide the outcome of a game. Increasingly, however, finance ministers have been letting in a lot of pucks, and the spenders have been scoring big. In other words finance ministers have not been making the strategic choices that their responsibilities of office demand.

The other watchdog is Treasury Board. The chief purpose of Treasury Board is to employ the federal public service, 240,000 strong, and by far the largest organization in the country. Or rather, Treasury Board represents the employer, the taxpayers of Canada. On the financial side, the responsibilities of Treasury Board centre on overseeing (1) the allocation of money to the spending departments to enable them to continue to implement existing programs at the same level of operation and (2) the allocation of new money for policy initiatives and new programs. The first category of financial resources is called in Ottawa the "A base." The inviolability of the A base is a key cog in the ratchet that makes the debt grow, as we shall see. In addition, of course, Treasury Board manages the enormous "human resource" through personnel policies, applying the Official Languages Act, co-ordinating the government planning process, and negotiating with public-service unions. It is a big job, and it is made even more difficult because the "employer" is constrained by a number of highly uneconomic social policies, of which the policy of official bilingualism, which requires the government to operate simultaneously in French and English, is the most notorious.

If Finance can be likened to a goalie, Treasury Board is akin to a score-keeper. The Secretariat of Treasury Board provides an account of who gets what money and of how many people, or person years (PYs) as they are called in Ottawa, will be allocated to the spending departments. The criteria for allocating PYs are, to say the least, flexible; and once new PYs have been allocated they automatically become part of the department's A base. Once part of the A base, PYs are harder to extract than molars from a mallard. Indeed, the universal watchword among officials is: don't touch the A base. For example, National Defence, with a $10-billion budget, asked for a supplementary allocation of $20,000 to cover the cost of special equipment needed to pro-

vide security for a papal visit. In principle, Treasury Board ought
to be able to say no. Normal common sense would dictate that
$20,000 could be reallocated somewhere from within a $10-bil-
lion budget. But that would mean touching the A base. Defence
got the extra cash.

The conclusion reached by many observers of how Ottawa
spends is that, in practice, the guardians turn out to be spenders
too. Finance, for example, is concerned with tax policy. The
budget speech is the main event for announcing changes in tax
policy and, given the requirements of budget secrecy, the minister of finance can formulate his tax policy pretty much on his
own. In doing so, he can (and does) have recourse to tax-expenditure accounts, popularly known as loopholes. Very simply,
loopholes amount to spending by not collecting. By 1980 there
were about 200 tax-expenditure items; by 1985 the list had
grown to 300. In some parts of the country there is a tax break
or even a direct subsidy for virtually every kind of commercial
activity. The Nielsen task force set up to review government programs concluded, for example, that there were 218 federal or
joint federal-provincial programs, costing $16.4 billion, and
68,000 PYs, designed to "help" the private sector. Many of these
were in the form of tax breaks. More to the point, it is virtually
impossible to determine the dollar amounts involved because
individual tax expenditures have an impact on one another. A
ballpark estimate, however, is that tax expenditures cost around
$30 billion annually. Businessmen take advantage of tax breaks
not because they need to but because the tax breaks are there. If
a businessman did not, he would be at a competitive disadvan-
tage because he would increase his risks or costs or both.

The ineffectiveness of Treasury Board as a watchdog is a
result of political considerations. Treasury Board is the oldest
committee of cabinet, having been established the day after
Confederation. But it is not the only cabinet committee to influence the expenditure budget. The Priorities and Planning Committee, in particular, has weakened both the power and prestige
of Treasury Board. Moreover, apart from the president, the

other members of Treasury Board are junior ministers who, naturally enough, aspire to be senior ministers. There are many ways for junior ministers to become senior ministers, but none involves opposing the desires of more powerful cabinet colleagues when they want to spend money, which is just about always. When there are only two half-hearted watchdogs and around thirty-five enthusiastic spenders, it is no surprise to learn that few junior ministers on Treasury Board take satisfaction in frustrating the spending proposals of ministers whose support they need for their own spending plans. When guardians become spenders their authority as trustees of the public purse evaporates. Without the strong support of the prime minister, neither Finance nor Treasury Board has much of a hope to rein in the high-flyers and big-spenders around the cabinet table. Not in living memory has Canada had a prime minister who was committed to anything but verbal exhortation in favour of fiscal restraint.

This brings us to the central problem of uncontrolled public spending. There have been two major royal commissions, the Glassco (1962) and the Lambert (1979), and two equally high-profile task forces, the Forget investigation of unemployment insurance (1986) and the Nielsen review of government programs (1986). All presented recommendations on how to cut expenditures; none has been acted upon. Governments have been elected on a platform of restraining expenditure and defeated when they failed. So the question remains: Why do governments spend the way they do? Why do the spenders always win and the guardians always lose?

One explanation, not wholly misleading, is to blame the bureaucracy. Individual civil servants have no incentives to cut spending when virtually all their personal and professional goals can be directly related to the size of the budget under their control. But this explanation must be balanced with a political one. Most ministers are incapable of changing existing policies even if they wanted to. And the fact is, most ministers lack both any interest in and any incentive for cutting programs and expenditures. It's much easier to add to both.

Consider the following case. You have just been named a cabinet minister. Your first task, after taking the oath of office, is to read through several large briefing books and listen to several more oral briefings by civil servants who are much more familiar with your ministry than you are. Probably they have more brains as well but are content to prove this indirectly, by letting you do what they want. Your deputy minister, who is very clever indeed, cannot be removed by you, and everyone else reports through him (or, conceivably, through her) and depends on him or her for promotions. Besides, as a cabinet minister, you are too busy to deal with department matters in any detail. There are cabinet meetings to go to and constituents and interest groups and caucus to meet. So you rely on your officials, especially your senior officials. You know you have begun to be part of the team when you realize that, instead of being suspicious of all public officials, you have discovered an exception: your own deputy minister. It's other departments that have the deadwood, the waste, and the inefficiencies, it seems, not yours.

For its part, the bureaucracy thinks of itself as permanent and of the minister as a political bird of passage. Bureaucrats know they have the power not simply because they outlast ministers and governments, but because they can so easily frustrate a bright-eyed, ambitious minister who wants to reform things by cutting expenditures. All they need to do is provide incomplete information, enter into collusion with one another, delay or create immediate deadlines, and control access. Their abilities to frustrate are limited only by their imaginations. By itself, the ethos of public-sector management stresses strict adherence to appropriate procedures and format. Benefits accrue to bureaucrats who do things by the book, not to those who rock the boat. The reason, again, is simple: process managers, as they are called, are easy to identify and easy to reward. Those who actually try to do something new, such as save money, will necessarily cause stress by disrupting the organized routine. This second kind of manager, usually called a "resource manager," is harder to identify and reward. The result is that process managers get promoted, and resource managers look like troublemakers.

Process managers have established uniform rules and regulations wherever possible, which means that the same procedures must be followed in different environments. This requirement inhibits any attempt at obtaining administrative efficiency that involves innovation. And all administrative reform involves innovation. The age profile of the civil service makes the introduction of new ways of doing things even more difficult. The largest cohort of bureaucrats, nearly 37 per cent, was between thirty-five and forty-four years old in 1990. This is a much larger percentage than the Canadian population in the same age group. This large group of middle-aged time-servers has a debilitating, even a deadening impact on effective administration. It sits like a huge plug in the pipe, stifling the ambitions of younger civil servants, whose opportunities for promotion are stymied. We may expect, therefore, that the resistance to innovation will increase as it becomes more difficult to rejuvenate the bureaucracy through the injection of new blood. Even if the government were serious about downsizing the civil service, under present rules and regulations, the last ones to go would be the longest serving, precisely the ones who resist innovation most strongly.

Possibly the most important administrative disincentive to saving money is the doctrine of "lapsing balances." Parliament approves funding for one fiscal year, and if financial resources are not spent they are unavailable the following year. Indeed, lapsing funds are considered to be evidence of bad planning and an inability to stick to a budget, not evidence of efficiency or frugality. And when funds are cut, there is no guarantee that they will stay in the same department, let alone under the control of a frugal manager. If you are a frugal bureaucrat you are not likely to remain one when you see taxpayers' money that you have saved being turned over to spendthrifts elsewhere, or worse, being turned over to a politician with a politically motivated boondoggle in mind. This is the bureaucratic version of the prisoner's dilemma faced by ministers.

Related to the problem of lapsing balances is another incentive for bureaucrats to manage badly, the fact that your own administrative promotion is often directly linked to the number of subordinate PYs reporting to you. The more people you supervise, the higher your classification and the greater your salary. If you can obtain ten PYs to do the job of two, you will be promoted to a higher classification. On the other hand, if you are an efficient manager and reduce your staff from ten to two you are likely to be rewarded with a demotion. Just as spending ministers always win over the guardians, so too do empire-building bureaucrats always win over prudent and frugal managers. In short, neither the politicians nor the civil service have any incentive at all to economize. Without the need to show profits and without the sting of competition, there is, in effect, no bottom line. In consequence, there is virtually no way to determine whether a bureau is performing well, notwithstanding the enormous array of evaluation criteria available and the congeries of committees, agencies, and offices to apply them. Evaluation consultants are part of the problem, not part of the solution.

It is entirely possible that, even without Quebec, Canada would have mired itself in this economic bog. And we are not saying that Quebec is alone responsible for the economic disorder of the entire country — though, as we shall see, the demands from the people and government of Quebec have contributed mightily to the present mess. The point of this survey of government mismanagement is first to indicate the extent of the crisis; our economic problems are a reality that will not go away. Second, however, it is our contention that, in the absence of Canada's ongoing constitutional crisis, at the heart of which is the Quebec question, Canada's leaders would have been able to face up to the economic difficulties of the country when they were still merely problems and not the crises they have become. Successive governments have been aware of the ever-mounting tide of red ink; they have even learned how to stem it, thanks to Forget, Neilsen, and the rest. But nothing has been done. To see why, one must consider the political engine driving the increase in economic disorder.

Considered in political isolation, it is reasonable enough for the spenders to be unconcerned with economizing. In order to get things done, to deliver programs, and transact the nation's business, it is necessary to spend money. Fair enough; but there is more to it than that. Politicians, and especially ministers, like to be remembered by the folks back home. It's always nice to have a bridge or a building named after you. And, of course, they also like to win the next election. The easiest way of doing both, they think, is to spend money. Since even the most exalted minister is elected locally, he or she must first take care of the constituents, and then the region. No cabinet minister has ever been fired for fighting too hard for his or her constituency or region, though several have quit because they said the government was not doing enough for the electors back home.

If politicians and bureaucrats have their version of prisoner's dilemma, it should be no surprise to learn that so too does the country at large. The usual term for it is regionalism. In an earlier day, when provincial governments were small and devoid of experts and others who claimed to be competent, at a time when it took days, not hours, to travel from Halifax or North Battleford to Ottawa, regional barons sat at the cabinet table and took care of their own. Even in more recent years it is no secret that ministers such as Allan J. MacEachen or Roméo LeBlanc were particularly adept at securing projects for their home regions. And even within regions the influence of powerful cabinet ministers can be felt. Despite the fact, for example, that most Japanese tourists who visit Alberta are more keen to visit Banff than West Edmonton Mall, the port of entry for direct flights from Japan is Edmonton, not Calgary. It has not gone unnoticed in Calgary that the minister of external affairs and the deputy prime minister in the Mulroney government were elected from constituencies near Edmonton. Strong regional ministers usually gain influential positions in cabinet and in turn are able to influence spending so as to assist their political base at home.

The Keynesian context for government expenditures exacerbates this "normal" political practice. In 1957 the Gordon Royal Commission on Canada's Economic Prospects introduced the fateful term "regional disparities." Ever since, governments have been pledged to alleviate or even remove these apparently terrible things. Occasionally, spokesmen for regions, usually premiers, get carried away and call upon the federal government not to rest until all provinces have economic performances above the national average. Only slightly less absurd, in 1981 the premier of Newfoundland called upon Ottawa to spend sufficiently in his province to ensure it would grow at twice the national average. It is not at all self-evident, however, that spending by the federal government, no matter how lavish, can significantly alter regional economic performances, at least not in the short run, which is the only perspective most political leaders can adopt.

When regional economic incentives were first introduced, no less an observer than Judy LaMarsh recalled that the results were simply disruptive. Communities competed with one another to show how poor they were, how low was their growth, how much they stood in need of government aid. When the prime minister of the day declared that only communities living in dire straits would qualify for a certain program, an enterprising Newfoundland village promptly changed its name to Dire Straits in the hope of finding a place at the trough. The same attitude prevailed in the House of Commons and, LaMarsh said, even more ferociously in the Liberal caucus. This is not to say that all regional economic policies are irrational. It is to say that it adds to the perversion of Keynesian double-talk because it separates (or "disaggregates," as the economists say) what Keynes required to be generalized or "aggregated." The promise of Keynes was for apolitical management of the economy; the result was its political mismanagement. Moreover, the biggest pigs got the most slops. This meant Ontario, since its economy was the biggest, and then Quebec, since its political squeals were the loudest. The result, again, was further to distort any rational economic development in the name of political expediency.

This does not mean, however, that political leaders draw the obvious conclusion — that allowing market forces to operate more freely would benefit the economy as a whole. It is conceivable that a government seriously concerned with reducing the debt might scrap its expensive attempt to keep people living in economically backward areas. It is not utter fantasy that the young and able-bodied pensioners of Cape Breton might leave home for a job in Prince George or Port Huron. After all, Goin' Down the Road was one of the small number of Canadian movies worth watching. To take a single specific example, why is it impossible to reform the unemployment-insurance program? After all, the Forget task force made an exhaustive analysis and came to some quite sensible conclusions. Why did the government forget Forget?

The simple answer is: Quebec. Canada's very generous unemployment-insurance policy, which is really a disguised form of welfare rather than a true insurance scheme, which has supported such bizarre phenomena as the UI Ski Team at Whistler, B.C., and which has been criticized by a succession of committees and commissions, benefits Quebec more than any other province. The Forget Report estimated that Quebec received $578 million more than it contributed to unemployment insurance. The logic of Quebec's position in the unemployment-insurance game is clear enough: if a Quebecker must leave his or her home province, and linguistic and cultural community — his or her "distinct society" — to find work, this is said to impose a greater hardship on him or her than would be suffered by a Newfoundlander migrating to Toronto. Or, if Newfoundlanders might find that example objectionable, it is certainly easier for an Albertan to go to British Columbia in search of work than it is for a Quebecker. Having a generous unemployment-insurance scheme makes it easier for Quebeckers to stay at home, unemployed and supported at public expense, than would otherwise be possible. One need not be a cold-hearted economist to conclude that this policy is as generous as it is not because Canadians are particularly in favour of elevated levels of welfare, but for political reasons. It would follow that Canada sans Quebec could very quickly and painlessly reduce current unemployment-insurance provisions.

The point of this example is not to raise the question of whether non-Quebeckers think it is "worth" paying $500 million a year to keep Quebeckers at home. The point is that an already misbegotten policy of using federal cash to attempt to alleviate regional disparities works to the greater comparative advantage of Quebec than of any other province. Rather than tinker at the margins in the hope of "stimulating" the local economy through government spending — that seems doomed to be perpetually unrealized — we should consider allowing natural market forces to work themselves through the economy. Unfortunately, current policy, which encourages people to stay unproductive and at home, breeds cynicism and despair. The only beneficiaries are short-sighted politicians who claim that by keeping their constituents at home and dependent on the government they are really helping them. Of course, the bureaucrats who supply all this "help" benefit too by holding down a job and by thinking they are doing good. But we do not share the view that citizens are ever really helped by being kept dependent upon government. We think that dependency breeds servility not self-reliance. And while some politicians might prefer the electorate to be servile, we do not think this is a civic virtue. Nor do we think that anyone in the civil service really benefits by having to deliver useless or harmful programs.

The only unambiguous consequence is that regional development programs have helped ratchet up the debt. Again the mechanism is simple. When the government is seen to have an obligation to do something to relieve economic imbalance, it does so initially in a limited target area. But the resources to help this small group of citizens come from the wallets of the general population. Non-designated groups invariably want to get in on the deal. It's another free lunch. And then the initially targeted group will want to have the programs expanded. And so will everyone else. The best illustration of this model case is the evolution of the Department of Regional Economic Expansion (DREE).

In 1968, Prime Minister Trudeau, with his usual flair for excess, declared that "economic equality is just as important as equality of language rights." To show how serious he was, he appointed his old pal Jean Marchand to run DREE. Marchand announced with great fanfare that DREE would spend 80 per cent of its budget east of Three Rivers, Quebec, in designated "growth areas," such as Moncton and St. John. Montreal-area MPs were quick to point out the obvious, that their city was the true growth area in the province but that, *hélas!*, it was not keeping up with expectations. Its unemployment rate was one-and-a-half times that of Toronto, even though it had elected more Liberals. The political logic of these facts pointed to an obvious conclusion: Montreal should be designated a special region. And it was, along with Hull and three Ontario counties. Marchand promised that this special "Region C" would exist for only two years. But then unemployment stayed high and the Parti Québécois was elected and Montreal had seven cabinet ministers. Political logic therefore demanded a new program, a discretionary-incentives program it was called, tailor-made for Montreal. But if Montreal received special treatment, why not Toronto or Vancouver?

And so DREE became DRIE, the Department of Regional Industrial Expansion, with a mandate to spend money everywhere in the country. The result was to ensure that the greatest amount of spending was done in the most powerful region, the Windsor-Quebec City corridor. By 1985, 70 per cent of DRIE funds were spent in Ontario and Quebec. Now it was time for Atlantic Canada and the West to complain. They had their own cabinet voices, and soon enough regional agencies were established. But how could we leave central Canada without subsidies? And so DRIE became DIST, the Department of Industry, Science and Technology, which could, of course, spend everywhere, but which would spend mainly in Ontario and Quebec. And so it goes.

All these programs fully conformed to the requirements of perverse Keynesianism. Elsewhere in the liberal and industrial world, notably in Britain and the United States, there has been a kind of anti-Keynesian backlash or at least a movement to query the previously self-evident wisdom of state intervention in the market, whether aggregated or not. In policy terms, it has taken the form of selling off or "privatizing" state-owned assets and enterprises.

In opposition, the Tories had been persistent critics of Crown corporations. Soon after becoming leader of the Conservative Party in 1983, Brian Mulroney appointed a five-person task force to look into the problem. It recommended selling off the major assets: Petro-Can, CN, AECL, and Air Canada. Michael Wilson's first budget promised action, and shortly thereafter it was announced that a raft of Crown corporations would soon be up for sale. After a certain amount of bungling, some of the smaller Crowns, such as Teleglobe and de Havilland, were sold. To avoid further mistakes, an Office of Privatization and Regulatory Affairs was established in 1986. If Crowns no longer served a public-policy function or if they were financially attractive, they would be prime candidates for privatization.

The two most obvious candidates were Air Canada and Petro-Canada, but others, such as CN Hotels and, the Toronto Harbourfront Corporation, were also included among the eligible. All that was needed was the right market conditions. Ever since the office was established to "guide" the privatization process, things have gone more slowly. That is, of course, one way to avoid making the sort of mistakes that were made early in the first Mulroney government. But it was also recognized that the market value of a major Crown such as Petro-Can was less than its book value. This meant that selling it off would actually increase the deficit.

There are other reasons why privatization has not proceeded apace, however. The minister of finance, for example, would like to see the assets of Crowns revert to his piggy bank, the Consolidated Revenue Fund. But the spending ministers insist that any funds generated stay with them. The proceeds from the 45 per cent share of Air Canada, for instance, went to purchase new airplanes. In the smaller Crown sales, Finance has prevailed, but the assets have hardly made a dent in the deficit. Even more important than the spenders' opposition to Finance is the fear by important ministers and regional caucuses of MPs that privatization would deprive their home turf of economic benefits and jobs, and that these benefits and jobs would not be replaced by the market. That is, opposition to privatization, pure and simple, is support for a local free lunch. But there is no free lunch. The rest of us pay for it.

A single example will do. Toronto Harbourfront Corporation owns a nice piece of high-priced real estate in downtown Toronto. Estimates of its value are upwards of $100 million. It was provided to the city as a reward or bribe during the 1972 election by Pierre Trudeau's Liberals. Now Conservative Toronto-area ministers insist it was a gift to the city and that it would be churlish to take it back and hand it over to "developers." Or, if it were to be privatized, the proceeds should be diverted to sustain cultural events and recreational activities for the good folks in Canada's wealthiest city. Ministers and MPs from beyond the golden horseshoe for some reason didn't see it the same way and accordingly made special-case requests to spare their own favourite Crowns. It was impossible to chop any because it was impossible to chop one. Whether it is a question of genuine spending initiatives or efforts to recoup assets through privatization, regional demands and political logic lead to uneconomic resource allocation. It has been this way for a generation.

And then there's language. Every Canadian knows that language has become a political issue today, but most of us are confused about why it is an issue and what, if anything, can be done about it. We can begin to sort things out with the recollection that language became a political issue in Canada when it became a political issue in Quebec. And that happened when the new middle class exhausted its opportunities in the unilingual public and quasi-public bureaucracies of the province. The success of the new middle class came when it gained control of the health, education, and welfare bureaucracies during the Quiet Revolution. In contrast, the private corporations were integrated into the national, the continental, and the world economy, all of which, by and large, operate in English. In other words, the economically productive bureaucracies — the private-sector bureaucracies that finance the expenditures of the health, education, and welfare bureaucracies — remained closed to French. By and large, clerical, administrative, and white-collar positions remained in the hands of the "English." The national and international corporations replied that the use of English made for greater efficiency. Whether this was true or not, it was clearly a self-serving response. In any event, the "greater-efficiency" argument did not convince the nationalists of Quebec's new middle class or the Government of Quebec that served its interests. Accordingly, it was a simple matter to pass the required language legislation. There was nothing particularly sinister or untoward in doing so. It simply reaffirmed what everyone knows on the basis of common sense: first, that governments serve the interests of those who elect them, and second, that language is territorial.

The denial of the last-mentioned fact — that language is territorial — is what makes official bilingualism either a waste or an irritant. Listening to the bilingual announcements of flights between Prince Rupert and Vancouver is, as journalist Peter Brimelow once remarked, analogous to the Irish peasants' custom of leaving bowls of milk on the doorstep for the "little people" with whom they believed they shared their island. The irritation is an expression not of an anti-French attitude but of impatience with a misbegotten policy. Since, in fact, language really is territorial, there is no way on God's green earth that, short of massive coercion, the government can "save" French linguistic communities outside Quebec. Premier Bourassa's recognition of this fact was clearly demonstrated by his remark in Edmonton in April 1988 that he was quite content with Saskatchewan's treatment of its French-speaking citizens, and that he was sure his good friend, Don Getty, would look after the French-speakers of Alberta.

Since the start of the Quiet Revolution Quebec governments have, for the most part, taken the attitude that the French outside Quebec are, for all practical purposes, lost sheep. That may or may not be true. What is true, however, is that the salvation of those communities outside Quebec lies in the hands of the communities themselves and of the men and women who make up those communities. Like all minorities everywhere in a democratic society, it is up to them alone to determine what degree of acculturation they will seek.

There are those who justify official bilingualism as a "lofty ideal." This may be so, and if it is, it amounts to a kind of *noblesse oblige.* What those who pursue lofty ideals forget, however, is that nobility *n'oblige que la noblesse.* The rest of us have to foot the bill, it seems, so those few with their lofty ideals can feel good about themselves. A less obnoxious version of this odd kind of *snobisme* is the assertion that Canadians are better off for having learned a second language. But official bilingualism has nothing to do with self-improvement: it is a doctrine that legally compels the Government of Canada to function in two languages at the same time. When that government takes 50 per cent of the GNP while only 7 per cent of English-speakers are fluent in French this fact has importance as an index of the skewed distribution of power. The other purpose of official bilingualism — to overcome the alleged alienation of Quebec from Canada — is also a joke. Or rather, it is worse than a joke: it is an insult. It is hard to imagine any Quebec politician, or indeed any member of the French nation in North America, making a moral or political virtue out of bilingualism. Only official-language commissioners are still labouring under that particular illusion.

As a kind of postscript we might make brief mention of the financial costs to the rest of the country of the clearly futile attempt to show the value of Confederation to Quebec. The direct costs of bilingualism, for example, can be calculated from public accounts estimates for the Department of the Secretary of State. Beginning in 1971, the figures for five-year intervals moved from less than half a billion in the 1971-75 period to more than a billion for the 1975-80 period. Growth continued for 1980-85 to nearly a billion and a half, and costs for 1985-90 have been estimated at around 2.3 billion dollars. On top of these admittedly impressive direct costs are the indirect costs to the economy incurred by businesses that have been persuaded to comply with government guidelines.

Official bilingualism is only the most blatant of a series of futile policy initiatives designed to retain the allegiance of Quebec. In addition, there is a whole range of expenditures, investments, and fiscal transfers that have aimed at obtaining the political loyalty of Quebec by directly stimulating the local economy. Some of these expenditures are part of the normal kinds of transfer that governments wedded to Keynesian doctrines are likely to undertake. Taxes collected in Quebec get circulated through Ottawa and returned to the province as expenditures by the federal government. In addition to what might be called normal or balanced fiscal accounts, the possibility exists for unbalanced ones as well. These are much more interesting. During the 1980 referendum debate, the federalist ministers from Ottawa mentioned some large numbers. André Ouellet said that the Canadian government spent more than $5 billion a year on wages, social assistance, subsidies, capital expenditures, guaranteed loans, and contracts; his colleague Marc Lalonde pointed out that as an independent country Quebec would be paying an additional $3.8 billion for oil. But that was just the tip of the iceberg.

It is a difficult but not impossible task to calculate whether one province is favoured. Robert L. Mansell and Ronald C. Schlenker of the Economics Department, University of Calgary, have done so for the period 1961-88, using data provided by Statistics Canada. Mansell and Schlenker provide annual estimates for what they called the regional allocation of net federal fiscal balances. This is a technical way of describing whether a province or region gets more than it gives. Specifically, "net federal fiscal balance" is defined as the total of all federal revenues (direct and indirect taxes, current transfers from persons, and investment income) minus federal expenditures in, and transfers to, that province or region. On the other side of the ledger are current expenditures on goods and services, transfer payments, interest on the public debt, and investment in fixed capital and inventories. When the net federal balance is positive it means that the combination of all federal tax and expenditure policies produces a net withdrawal from the economy of the region or province. From the perspective of Ottawa, a positive balance can be viewed as a net contribution by the province to the financing of federal government activities. Conversely, a negative balance means a net injection to the economy of the region or province. Mansell and Schlenker are concerned only with direct effects.

From time to time, political pundits make the point that Quebec and the West have a lot in common, that they are natural political allies against Ottawa or against Ontario. One hears stories of how well Peter Lougheed and René Lévesque got along. These stories may even be true. It is certainly true that the populations of the West and Quebec are about the same size. When we look at fiscal balances, however, it is the differences not the similarities that stand out.

Consider the following data comparing Quebec and the West, and remember that the West includes two "have-not" provinces, Saskatchewan and Manitoba, where federal government expenditures far exceed revenues. For the period 1961-88, the federal government spent about $136 billion more in Quebec than it removed. In the West, it removed about $100 billion more than it spent. And if you just look at Alberta and British Columbia, it took a whopping $155 billion more in revenue than it spent. On a per-capita basis, every Quebecker got $757 a year over the 1961-88 period and every westerner paid about $795. When we look at the period after the first PQ victory in 1976, the price paid by westerners stayed about the same, $750 a head. But every Quebecker received $1565. One need not be a cynic nor always expect the worst from government to conclude that the federal government was spending money in order to purchase the loyalty of Quebec. It didn't work.

Earlier in this chapter we pointed out that after the mid-1970s — about the same time that the PQ won its first victory — the federal government became incapable of managing its expenditure budget and in consequence began to run significant annual deficits. When the deficit is taken into account, the results are even more significant: the federal balance with Quebec is about $63 billion in Quebec's favour. On a per-capita basis, every Quebecker has received about $816 per year; every westerner has paid $572. When Alberta and British Columbia alone are considered, the figures move in the expected directions.

We have said already that Quebec is not the cause of this perverse policy. Other regional demands and other provincial demands would no doubt have helped the debt grow. We are not trying to single out Quebec and blame Quebeckers for playing the game. We are, however, saying that the game must be changed, that the country can't afford to play any more. We are also saying that Quebec has had an unjust advantage because its economic demands were also immediately understood as political. The implicit logic that has given every demand from Quebec more political weight than identical demands from, say, Manitoba, is the threat of separation. This was transparently clear in the decision to award the CF-18 repair contract to a Montreal not a Winnipeg firm, despite the demonstrably better terms offered by the Winnipeg company.

We have said we are not blaming Quebec and we mean it. But we are not about to overlook the consequences of the Quebec problem either. Undue attention to the political demands of that province — demands that, we believe, can never be met — have hurt the rest of the country. So far, the costs have simply been economic. Tomorrow they may be political as well.

Political Consequences

When we sit down to take stock of the performance of the Government of Canada over the past generation or so, we have to start somewhere. We started with the economy and government ineptness in attempting to manage it. The mistakes are easy to see and the arguments are clear. By according pride of place in the catalogue of errors to the economy, we are not being economic determinists. We are simply saying that economic policy is very important, that the government has botched it, and that it has done so for misguided political reasons, chief among them being the hope of bribing Quebec to abandon its aspirations to independence. The political fallout is clear from the record low levels of support that the public has given to the Mulroney government. It ought to be clear that a citizen whose loyalty can be bought is unworthy of his or her citizenship. Any Quebecker with an ounce of pride would reject any attempt to purchase his or her loyalty. One might expect Quebec nationalist sentiments to grow, not decline, in response to such a strategy. Even more to the point, how could non-Quebeckers do anything but look with contempt upon those who sold their birthright for a CF-18 contract?

This does not mean, of course, that governments have no need to deliver programs that citizens need, or perhaps merely want. No one in this country is so naive as to think governments survive purely on the basis of goodwill. On the contrary, leadership in Canada depends on credibility and cash. When the government is out of cash, its credibility and support evaporate. Forty years ago Canada was a model of fiscal probity; now, owing to years of mismanagement, we are heading towards a sharp reduction in our economic standard of living. Our choices are being restricted, and the opportunities to take action in order to resolve our current economic and political mess are growing more remote. Debt-servicing costs (which are high and are paid first) and an inability or unwillingness by ministers and bureaucrats to control spending or to introduce cost-effective administrative measures mean that the government has little scope to reallocate expenditures to deal with real current problems or, more importantly, future ones that the nation will inevitably have to face. These range from such marginal and perhaps non-existent issues as the greenhouse effect and the depletion of the ozone layer, issues over which Canada has in fact very limited control (even though Canadians are filled with care for these matters), to such obvious and central issues as education, research and development, and industrial modernization. Canada has become, in effect, the welfare bum of international research and development. Our educational system has become chronically underfunded, and parts of our industrial plant invite comparison with newly liberated sectors of the former Soviet empire. An increasingly large number of Canadians know it and have withdrawn their confidence from the federal government and from federal institutions. We have seen this not merely in the growing sentiment in favour of independence in Quebec but also, as mentioned earlier, in the constitutional agenda passed by the four western premiers at their conference in Lloydminster in the summer of 1990. These and other initiatives have not gone unnoticed in Ottawa, but the government clearly is at a loss about how to respond. Enjoying neither the confidence of the citizens nor enough cash to tackle the real and pressing problems of our future as a nation, government in Ottawa has become increasingly paralysed, even moribund. This is why association with Brian Mulroney is the kiss of death for any provincial premier.

The post-Meech sense of national disintegration has provided mischievous and ambitious politicians in the provinces, and especially in Quebec, with an unprecedented window of opportunity to advance their own agendas. After years of insensitivity in Ottawa to the problems of the West, western premiers at least have an intelligible interest in demanding more power. Even the Atlantic provinces seem ready to break the ties to Ottawa that have kept them dependent pensioners for generations. In both instances, the new boldness is fostered by an awareness that

Ottawa is unable to deliver. The same argument does not hold for Quebec. Far from having its interests ignored, Quebec has effectively set the political and constitutional agenda for the past quarter-century. Given that the federal government's options are severely restricted owing to its fiscal ineptness and bungling, we have a made-in-Canada recipe for political as well as economic disaster.

Here an anecdote is worth several thousand words of analysis. When he was a young reporter for the *Financial Post*, journalist Peter Brimelow interviewed Joe Clark. The year was 1975 and Clark was running for the leadership of the Conservative Party. Brimelow began by asking Clark for his opinion on the recently released Economic Council of Canada's report, *Looking Outward*. It had recommended free trade with the United States and had, naturally enough, been roundly denounced by many of the same self-appointed defenders of Canadian "nationalism" as were to denounce the Free Trade Agreement twenty years later. Clark replied that he really didn't know much about economics. "You see," he told the incredulous Brimelow, "when I went into politics I had to choose between learning economics and learning French." The future prime minister and minister of external affairs clearly made the right choice so far as his own career was concerned. But was the choice good for the country?

In the nature of things, politics is bound to be more important than economics. But that does not mean that learning French is more important than learning economics. It is more important only in Canada, and solely because of Quebec; or rather, because the existence of Quebec within Canada has provided generations of political entrepreneurs with the opportunity to manipulate an ethnic, cultural, and linguistic division.

For example, it has become a political necessity for the leader of any political party to be bilingual. This effectively makes Quebec the only pool of available candidates for prime minister. When Joe Clark won the leadership of the Conservative Party in 1976 it was a consequence, at least in part, of great good fortune. It is sometimes forgotten that he won over two Quebeckers, Brian Mulroney and Claude Wagner. When Brian Mulroney won in 1983 his ability to speak fluent French was his chief (perhaps his only) political asset. He had never been elected or even fought an election prior to his selection as leader of the Tories. When far more experienced politicians, such as John Crosbie, raised doubts about the necessity of being bilingual, they were roundly castigated in both official languages. The truth of the matter is, Crosbie was right. It is in no way self-evident that the ability to pass as a member of the French- or English-speaking community is a political virtue. It is a capacity shared with chameleons not statesmen.

In this respect, there is no difference between the Liberals and the Conservatives, except in style. The Liberals had the prudence to groom Pierre Trudeau for a year as a cabinet minister before they made him leader. More recently, the leadership race in the Liberal Party between Jean Chrétien and Paul Martin ensured that the Liberals too would be led by a Quebecker. (By this criterion Martin would have been preferable because he, like Trudeau and Mulroney, is accentless in the two languages.) The consequences are clear: by making bilingualism and cultural hermaphroditism major criteria for political leadership we have managed to exclude huge numbers of Canadians from the pool of potential leaders. By artificially reducing the number of possible leaders we have enhanced our current leadership crisis.

We may conclude this chapter with the following observation. By focusing so intently on the place of Quebec in the nation, the last generation of Canadian political leaders has provided us with a chronic constitutional crisis. This crisis has made it all but impossible to address the truly significant problems we face now and will inevitably face tomorrow in an even worse form. Many of these problems are simply consequences of uncontrolled and evidently uncontrollable public expenditures. Failure to address these real problems has further eroded the confidence of Canadians in their government. Lapsing confidence has made it even more difficult to address the ongoing constitutional crisis. Vicious circle or prisoner's dilemma, we are in a splendid mess from which extraction will be both costly and difficult. Like the moribund Soviet Union, we are in need of *novoye myshleniye* — "new thinking." In the chapters that follow we provide some, by sketching the course of Canada-Quebec relations.

2

TWO CANADAS

René Lévesque remembered that night as long as he
lived:

> There were tears and laughter, kisses and shouting.
> In our "secret" committee room . . . the ceiling
> threatened to come down, and I thought that was what had hap-
> pened when a heavy, dull thud was heard at the back of the
> room. It was our chief organizer who had just passed out, stiff as a
> board. The tension had been too much for him.

It was June 22, 1960. Jean Lesage's Liberals had won the Quebec
provincial election, ending sixteen years of rule by the ultra-
right Union Nationale party. Within days, Lévesque was to be
sworn in as Quebec's new minister of public works. The Quiet
Revolution had begun.

The victory of the Lesage Liberals set in train a series of
events that have not yet reached their climax. The Quiet Revolution initiated a period of profound change in Quebec, change
that would bring Quebeckers fully into the modern world and
that would eventually cause some of them to renew age-old calls

for independence. From the night of June 22, 1960, to now, Quebec has set the agenda for the evolution of Canadian federalism. That night the struggle of the French of Quebec to survive as a small minority in the middle of a continent of English-speaking Canadians and Americans entered a new phase: but, as with most historic events, the novelty was more apparent than real.

The French have struggled to survive in America from the very beginnings of European exploration and settlement. The British colony of Jamestown was the first permanent European habitation north of the Rio Grande, and the *Habitation* established by Samuel de Champlain in 1608 was the second. Although the English and the French began to colonize North America at roughly the same time, the English did a better job of it. The French seemed unable to make up their minds about what they wanted to do in America — to trade in furs or to clear land for farms and villages and the settlers that would people them. In fact, the two kinds of economic activity were not compatible; if farmers cut down the forests, they removed the habitat for fur-bearing animals and threatened the Indians, who were apt to resist. Agriculture posed a direct threat to their land and an indirect one to their place in the fur trade.

The settlers from the British Isles — we'll call them "the English," with apologies to the Welsh, Irish, and Scottish — were more single-minded, even though they were divided by religion, class, and occupation. To them America was a place to escape from religious persecution, to amass wealth, and to create a more egalitarian society. They came to America by the hundreds of thousands; the French came by the hundreds.

When England and France embarked on a series of wars for control of the continent — wars that in North America were sideshows to conflicts that raged around the globe — the French colonists did have certain advantages over the English. They were more united, by virtue of having the same religion and having come from the same areas of France. They lived in a small, compact colony that stretched primarily from the Saguenay River to the Island of Montreal (although French fur-trade posts and forts dotted the continental interior). They were far better at the art of war — having struggled for decades against the Iroquois — than were the English colonists. The English who lived in the fourteen British colonies, by contrast, were spread up and down the eastern seaboard and from the Atlantic coast to the foothills of the Appalachians. They were largely isolated from one another. They were divided by religion, occupation, and regional rivalry. But they had one overall advantage, and it was bound to tell sooner or later; by the outbreak of the last round of fighting (1754), they outnumbered the French by almost thirty to one!

The battle that took place on the Plains of Abraham, just to the west of the city walls of Quebec, on the morning of September 13, 1759, has been called "the most decisive in Canadian history." But like that of many other historical events, its significance has been exaggerated. It is certainly true that in that battle a contingent of British soldiers led by General Wolfe defeated a contingent of French, French-Canadian, and Indian troops led by General Montcalm. It is also true that the British Army then occupied Quebec City, which, situated as it was at the narrowing of the St. Lawrence River, controlled the supply routes from France to New France. That effectively ended the war in America. The famous "conquest," however, needs to be demythologized in two significant respects. First, the transfer of New France to Britain was only marginally influenced by the relatively insignificant battle of 1759. If Montcalm had prevailed on the field of honour, it is likely that Quebec would still have ended up British, because France was by no means reluctant to part with Quebec. The Treaty of Paris, 1763, ended a world-wide war. By its terms, France ceded its colony along the St. Lawrence to the British Empire, along with Cape Breton and Acadia, retaining only the islands of St. Pierre and Miquelon. The British reluctantly restored to France five islands: Guadeloupe, Martinique, Belle Isle, Maria Galante, and St. Lucia. More importantly, though an exchange of territory had taken place, the French presence in America was by no means extinguished.

The British Army, aided by British colonists and their Indian allies, had conquered New France; but to "conquer" the French colonists, a flood tide of English settlers would be needed. If French culture and the Roman Catholic religion were to be extinguished in Quebec, it could be done only by denying the French Catholic population the legal means to survive and by overwhelming it with English-speaking Protestant immigrants. The British briefly tried to do so but, in the years immediately after the cession, few English-speaking settlers came to Quebec. When tensions grew between the British and their American colonists — tensions that ultimately exploded into the American Revolution in 1775 — the British decided to try to win the French colonists over. They did this by passing the Quebec Act in 1774. The act confirmed the civil code of France in the colony (though it also established British criminal law) and extended a large degree of religious freedom to Catholics, though it did not give them the vote (Catholics in Britain were denied any religious rights at that time). The act also continued the old landholding system of New France — the "seigneurial system" — upon which, the British wrongly thought, the prestige and wealth of the local landed gentry were based. It was Britain's belief that these men — the seigneurs — and the Catholic church would be won over by the Quebec Act, especially since the act also barred the establishment of an elected legislative assembly in the colony. This last provision ensured that the handful of English colonists who had settled in Quebec since the conquest would not dominate the French, who could not vote for assembly members. For the moment, British policy seemed to assure the French that they would survive in America.

Although tens of thousands of loyal English-speaking immigrants came north following the American Revolution of 1775-83, few settled amongst the French. They went, instead, to Nova Scotia or to western Quebec. The latter group chafed under the

Quebec Act and demanded English civil law, an English (or rather colonial American) landholding system, and an elected assembly. In 1791 the British responded with the Constitutional Act, which split Quebec into two colonies — Upper Canada (now Ontario) and Lower Canada (now Quebec). Each colony would have an elected legislature. Upper Canada would have English laws and landholding provisions; Lower Canada would have French civil law and the seigneurial system. Both colonies would also have an upper house, appointed by the British governor, and an executive council — like a cabinet — also appointed by the governor. The stage was set for the French-English conflict in North America.

Although the French of Lower Canada had the vote and vastly outnumbered the English who lived there, the colony was dominated by the British governor and a small supporting clique, virtually all of whom were English. They were predominantly members of the Quebec City and Montreal business community, which was making a fortune in the northwestern fur trade and which wanted to invest the profits of that trade in shipping, banking, brewing, and other pursuits designed to bring even greater wealth to themselves and prosperity to the country at large. Like many businessmen before and since, they sought government help. They thought of the French as a backward, primitive, and superstitious people, dominated by the church and led by men — the seigneurs and the clergy — who neither understood nor sympathized with the needs of business.

And, in fact, the French *were* dominated by the seigneurs and by the church. Following the conquest, there were few other natural leaders. Few successful French businessmen had emerged prior to the cession of New France to Britain; most successful businessmen had been in the fur trade, which was now dominated by the English. The church's power had been augmented by the Quebec Act (which gave it a status it had never had in New France), as had the authority of the seigneurs, who had been little more than land agents before the British arrived. The church wanted its flock to "render unto Caesar the things that are Caesar's; and unto God the things that are God's." British power gave the church its position as educator; minister; comforter of the sick; registrar of births, deaths, and marriages; and overall distributor of welfare to the people. Its hierarchy was antidemocratic, antiliberal, antirepublican, anticapitalist.

In the first decades of the nineteenth century, the struggle between the English and French intensified in Lower Canada. A series of economic disasters made matters worse, as did the growth in English-speaking immigration and an increase in sales by French land-owners to English-speaking farmers. Central to the struggle was the issue of who would control the colony: the English-speaking minority, supported by the British, or the French majority, represented in the legislature by the Parti patriote led by seigneur Louis-Joseph Papineau. Papineau and his followers believed it was a struggle for nothing less than the survival of the French people in Canada. If the French were to lose, he reasoned, the English would flood the colony with English-speaking immigrants, grab French farm lands, and use French tax monies to consolidate the economic and political power of the English community. In the fall of 1837, he led his followers into armed revolt.

The Rebellions of 1837 were seminal events in the history of Canada. Increasingly frustrated by the unwillingness of the British to allow the will of the people to prevail over that of the English-speaking élite, Papineau sought to establish in Lower Canada an independent French republic based on many of the democratic ideals of the United States. His objective was not far different from that of the Upper Canada rebel William Lyon Mackenzie, who tried unsuccessfully, at virtually the same time, to launch a rebellion of his own against British rule. Papineau was supported by a handful of English-speaking liberals who shared his vision of a democracy astride the St. Lawrence River. Fighting raged at several locations near Montreal in November and December 1837 before the uprising was finally crushed by the British Army. Papineau fled to the United States, and Lord

Durham was dispatched to Canada from Britain to conduct an investigation into the causes of the uprisings.

In Durham's famous phrase, he found "two nations warring in the bosom of a single state" and proceeded to make recommendations that would set matters right. He was a liberal and a member of the new entrepreneurial class that had risen to wealth and prominence in Britain during the Industrial Revolution. Thus he had little sympathy for the conservative, Catholic, agricultural French and, like the English-dominated Lower-Canadian business community, he thought of them as a backward people, unschooled and uneducable in the ways of British liberty. Indeed, according to Durham, it was precisely the backwardness of the *habitant* that allowed him to be led into rebellion by the disgruntled élite. If Papineau and the other leaders had been granted a role in government commensurate with their wealth and talent and position, Durham reasoned, the rebellion never would have occurred. The solution to the disorders in both colonies was, therefore, clear to him: first Upper and Lower Canada should have a more democratic form of government, and second, the two colonies should be joined, giving English-speaking colonists from both sections a majority of seats in the new, combined, colonial legislature. It was Durham's view that the French must either be left alone entirely or be liberalized and assimilated. The rebellion was clear evidence that they had not been left alone, that they could not be left alone. The option of assimilating the French to a liberal and homogeneous society therefore recommended itself. It is for this reason that Durham has had such a mixed reception at the hands of Canadian historians. By and large they have applauded his attempts to democratize and liberalize the colonial society of British North America; but at the same they have condemned his apparent intolerance of French cultural diversity. In Durham's view, assimilation was the only means to obtain both prosperity and political harmony. It is not completely clear that he was wrong; it is clear that assimilation has proved to be impossible.

The democratic reforms Durham recommended did not

come until after 1846, but the unification of the colonies took place almost immediately. In 1841 the British passed the Act of Union, which joined Upper and Lower Canada to create the United Province of Canada. Assimilation, we know, was another matter. The French were simply too numerous and, more important, as government became more democratic in the 1840s, their votes and their support became crucial to the survival of any ministry. The long march of political compromise had begun.

During the three decades between the Rebellions of 1837 and Confederation in 1867, French Canadians became the single most important element in the Canadian political system. Papineau had believed that French-Canadian survival could be guaranteed only through independence. After a brief exile in the United States, he returned to Canada in 1844 to continue to preach his republican and separatist message. He gathered around him a group of young, liberal followers who formed the core of what became a radical, anticlerical party known as the Parti rouge.

But Papineau now had a rival, or rather, several rivals, who preached quite a different message. The most important of these leaders was Louis-Hippolyte LaFontaine, a one-time follower of Papineau, but a man who had opposed the uprising in 1837. Unlike Papineau, LaFontaine believed that the key to French-Canadian survival was political power within the government of the colony. If French votes were wisely cast, he thought, and if French political leaders were canny in their choice of coalition partners, then French Canadians would become indispensable to any government, especially since English-speaking colonists were divided by religion, ethnic and national origin, occupation, etc. Thus he made common cause with English-speaking reformers such as Robert Baldwin in the fight for truly democratic government in the colony.

In one way LaFontaine and Papineau represented the two poles of French-Canadian political thinking. LaFontaine believed that separation would lead to disaster because French

Canadians were a small minority in America; Papineau believed that separation was the only road to survival. LaFontaine believed that French-Canadian survival would be guaranteed both by French Canada's English-speaking coalition partners and by an astute use of the British parliamentary system; Papineau believed that French Canadians would be overwhelmed if they stayed within the British orbit. What they had in common was a fervent nationalism. Both Papineau and LaFontaine were nationalists who strongly believed that French Canada had a right to protect its collective identity and a duty to marshal its resources to ensure its survival.

That dichotomy — between the nationalists of the Papineau stripe and those of the LaFontaine variety — has marked French-Canadian politics and intellectual life ever since.

The coalition of French- and English-speaking reformers that Baldwin and LaFontaine pioneered governed Canada in the late 1840s and early 1850s, but tension grew when the population of the western, English-speaking section surpassed that of the eastern, primarily French-speaking section. Led by anti-Catholic radical reformers, the English-speaking colonists pressed for "rep by pop" — representation by population. That would have given the English-speaking areas more seats in the colony's legislature. The French felt threatened once again. Thus deadlock developed in the government of the colony. There were four parties in the legislature and none could gain a majority in the elections. In 1864, the leader of the English-speaking radicals, George Brown of Toronto, proposed a daring solution not only to the deadlock, but also to other problems then threatening the British North American colonies: he sought to create a coalition of parties to work for a federal union. His Conservative rival, John A. Macdonald, and the leader of the French-Canadian Conservatives, George-Etienne Cartier, both accepted. The Confederation of 1867 was the fruit of this coalition.

Confederation has usually been viewed by Canadians as a great coming-together of the British-American colonies. On one level, it was certainly that. On July 1, 1867, Nova Scotia, New Brunswick, and the colony of Canada were joined into the Dominion of Canada with one federal government and four provinces — Nova Scotia, New Brunswick, Quebec, and Ontario. Manitoba joined (after the Red River Rebellion, led by Louis Riel) in 1870, British Columbia in 1871, and Prince Edward Island in 1873. But Confederation was also as much a divorce as it was a marriage. The colony of Canada was split into two parts — a predominantly English-speaking Ontario and a predominantly French-speaking Quebec — so that each group could pursue its own destiny within the larger Dominion. There was opposition to Confederation in Quebec (as there was in the Maritimes and at Red River), but it was overcome largely through Cartier's emphasis on the fact that the provincial government of Quebec would have whatever powers were necessary — over schooling, language, civil law, etc. — to guarantee French-Canadian survival. Thus Quebec was to become the national government of French Quebeckers in all but name. In this respect, Confederation was an effort to combine the approaches of Papineau and LaFontaine.

Although Quebec was certainly intended to become the state charged with special responsibility to preserve French distinctiveness, Confederation was not a union of "two founding peoples" or the coming together of two "states." The Canada of 1867 was a diverse place. Protestant and Catholic Irish were bitter enemies in religion and politics and pummelled each other regularly in the streets of most large towns. Conservative, Scottish-born businessmen in cities such as Kingston or Montreal fought the radical, liberal, Freemason, Scottish-born farmers from western Ontario for political power. Maritimers feared and were suspicious of "upper" Canadians. And so it went. By no stretch of the imagination can one speak of unity in English-speaking Canada. There was a more or less common language, a more or less common fear (or envy) of the Americans; but that was all that brought these so-called English Canadians together.

Confederation was not, therefore, in any way a "coming

together" of French and English; nor was it a creation of the British colonies that had preceded it. In the first instance many, if not most, of the people in those colonies had been either hostile, or indifferent, to Confederation. They had to be cajoled, threatened, bribed, or fooled into acquiescence by colonial politicians who thought that Confederation would solve their problems. There had also been a tremendous amount of British pressure, thinly disguised in some cases, more naked in others, designed to ensure that London's message came through loud and clear: London was moving out of North America for its own reasons and British Americans had better learn to cohabit if they did not want the Americans moving in. Even if the colonies had been four-square in favour of Confederation, however, they could not have brought it about; as colonies, they had no legal or constitutional power to unite on their own. The act of unification had to be British, legislated by the British Parliament at Westminster, and proclaimed by Queen Victoria, if it was to have any legal force.

French-speaking and English-speaking supporters of Confederation had wanted to create Canada for very different reasons; Canada was a marriage of convenience, a business arrangement between very distinct partners, not a love-match. It is true that both societies were fundamentally conservative, but conservatism, unlike liberalism, is more a response to events than a plan for action. So far as the two Canadian societies were concerned, the historical reasons for their conservatism, namely the abandonment of the colony by France and the exile of the United Empire Loyalists, were quite distinct. In other matters they had little in common and could not agree on a unified set of principles upon which a united nation could be built. One good example was in the role of religion in daily life — something that counted for a great deal in the nineteenth century. In Quebec the Catholic church ministered to the needs of the people in matters both spiritual and temporal. The church played an active role in politics. In rural parishes it performed many of the civil functions that municipalities performed in Ontario. It was responsible for virtually all schooling. It was, for all intents and purposes, an official state religion.

Nothing of the kind existed in Ontario, where the multiplicity of Protestant denominations had led most political (and religious) leaders to conclude as far back as the 1830s that the state should favour no denomination. That brought Ontario much closer to the church-state separation that was a key feature of the U.S. Constitution than to the church-state relationship that existed in its neighbour province to the east. With such different approaches to as basic a matter as the role of religion in the state, how could these two language groups arrive at a common concept of nation? Quite simply, they did not. This is why virtually every great enterprise that was embarked upon by "Canadians" after 1867 was launched by either one or the other of these language groups, but almost never by both acting together. Put another way, those things that were important to English-speaking Canadians — settlement of the West, industrialization, playing a significant part in the two world wars — were not important to francophone Quebeckers.

The separate aspirations of English-speaking and French-speaking Canadians was manifest soon after Confederation. English-speaking Canada was quickly preoccupied with transcontinental expansion, western settlement, industrial development, the construction of a railway to the Pacific — with the creation of institutions to develop a common national character. The active participation of the French was not needed for many of these aims to be achieved. It was not particularly wanted either. English-speaking Canada turned out to be more successful than many might have expected. By the turn of the century the aboriginal peoples of the West had been shunted aside. Millions of immigrants were settling the West and breaking prairie sod, carried there on the transcontinental CPR. Great factories in Ontario, Quebec, and even the Maritimes were turning out an immense assortment of manufactured products, protected from foreign competition by high tariffs.

While Ontario farmers, workers, and entrepreneurs, Quebec industrialists (mostly English-speaking), and Maritime loggers, fishermen, and bankers attempted to build a modern industrial state, most Quebeckers were moving in another direction. Their intellectual, political, and religious leaders believed that Quebec's survival as a distinct society could be guaranteed only by the maintenance and protection of Quebec's insularity. They believed that if the people of Quebec emulated the rest of North America's pursuit of material prosperity through entrepreneurship, profits, and technological advancement, Quebec would lose its Catholic heart and its rural, conservative soul. They made little effort to play a role in westward expansion. In fact, French Quebeckers were dissuaded from joining the trek west, claiming that if they did so they would lose touch with the larger francophone community and would be in danger of losing their French and Catholic identities in the bargain. Since Quebec had insufficient land and too few jobs to sustain its population, hundreds of thousands of French-Canadian men and women who needed bread more than religious succour or French culture emigrated anyway. They went to the mill towns of New England to work, to settle, and, eventually, to lose their French identity forever in the American melting-pot.

The existence in Canada of two linguistic groups, one French, the other English, made it impossible for Canada even to begin to grow from a collection of disparate colonies spread across a continent into a nation. The late Frank Underhill, one of Canada's most perceptive historians, tackled the question of what would have constituted Canadian nationhood in a series of lectures delivered in 1963. He defined "nation" this way: "a body of people who have done great things together in the past and who hope to do great things together in the future." If we are to take that as a working definition of nationhood, Canada did not and does not measure up. Canada is not, in his sense, a nation, because the two significant groups in Canadian life have always been out of step with each other. Canadians are not, in Underhill's words, a body of people; we have never been a body politic.

Some English-speaking Canadians tried to create a sense of nationhood from the very beginning of Confederation. The Canada First movement was a small group of intellectuals and journalists who tried to design a Canadian nationalism. They took the then-current tradition of European nationalism as their model and made much of the impact of the northern climate on Canadian behaviour. To the Canada First movement we owe the concept of Canada as the "true north, strong and free." Although most were liberal, and therefore strongly anti-Catholic, they even tried to include French Canada in their definitions, stressing the common Norman ethnicity in the origins of both the French Canadians and the British immigrants. They failed dismally. Designer nationalism could not create a national character because no single definition of "Canadian" could possibly encompass those who spoke French as well as those who spoke English. The differences stemmed not simply from a different way of speaking, but from different world views nourished by quite distinct historical, cultural, religious, and political experiences.

From Confederation until the mid-1880s an uneasy truce of sorts settled over French-English relations in Canada. No major disputes over language, religion, schooling, or the basic direction of the country broke out. Although both Manitoba and the North-West Territories assumed a temporary bilingual character as a result of the bargain struck between the Red River Métis and John A. Macdonald at the time of the Red River Rebellion in 1869-70, that bilingualism was nothing more than a reflection of the population mix in the west in the 1860s and 1870s. During those years, at least 50 per cent of westerners were the French-speaking and Catholic descendants of mixed marriages between native women and fur traders. But because few Quebeckers settled there, the French were soon greatly outnumbered by English-speaking settlers who eventually decided to impose their own vision of a unilingual, unicultural society on the West. This was a major contributing factor to the breakdown in the French-English truce, one that, for the first time, brought the two fundamentally different conceptions of Canada held by French- and English-speaking Canadians into conflict with each other.

A number of closely related events, beginning with the North-West Rebellion of 1885, brought French-English conflict to the fore. In 1885 Louis Riel again led the Métis against the government in Ottawa. This time the rising was centred in the valley of the North Saskatchewan River. The rebellion was crushed; Riel was captured, tried for treason, found guilty, and condemned to be hanged. Though Quebec had not supported Riel — he had turned against the Catholic church in the years since the 1869 rebellion — many Quebeckers took pity on him following his trial and demanded clemency on the grounds that the negligence of the federal government had created the conditions that provoked the Métis to rebel. There was more than a little identification with the defeated Métis as a fellow "oppressed" (or simply misunderstood) minority. There was even some thought that the execution of Riel was somehow a blow at French rights in the West — a patent absurdity. In Ontario, by contrast, Riel was depicted by press, politicians, and Protestant religious leaders as a messianic and bloodthirsty killer who deserved no mercy.

Macdonald was caught in a bind. He personally believed in Riel's guilt and in the appropriateness of the death sentence. But he was well aware that, whatever Riel's fate, one community or the other would be politically alienated and aggrieved. Eventually he decided; Riel would hang "though every dog in Quebec bark in his favour." Hang he did, and the lesson of his execution was not lost on Quebec's leaders: when the English-speaking majority decided to act as one, the French-speaking minority would be defeated every time. To Quebeckers, Riel's hanging became a symbol of Quebec's minority status and its subservient place in Confederation.

Riel's execution was a major factor in Honoré Mercier's election as premier of Quebec in 1886. Mercier headed Quebec's first "nationalist" government; he aimed to enhance provincial power and orient French Canadians primarily towards Quebec City. He found his foil in Wilfrid Laurier, a former nationalist of Parti rouge stripe, who was elected leader of the federal Liberal Party in 1887. Laurier was LaFontaine to Mercier's Papineau. Laurier believed that French interests could ultimately be defended only in Ottawa. In the 1870s, at considerable risk to his political career, he had taken on the clerical leaders of Quebec who had tried to forge a Catholic-Conservative alliance. Such an alliance, he had claimed, would prompt English-speaking Protestant Canadians to forge a religious-political alignment of their own. When that happened, French Canadians as a group would be placed in a permanent minority status in Canada and would be forever powerless.

Laurier did not achieve power until 1896. Until then, Mercier was the political leader of French Canada. In 1887 he played host to the premiers of Manitoba, Ontario, Nova Scotia, and New Brunswick at Quebec City. This first Interprovincial Conference had actually been called by Ontario premier Oliver Mowat, who needed allies in his own battles with the federal government. Mowat and Macdonald were bitter rivals; more than that, however, Mowat wanted to increase the provinces' ability to determine the future of their own urban and industrial development. It was he who used this conference to enunciate the "compact theory of Confederation" — the fanciful notion that Canada had been created by sovereign provinces coming together at Confederation. In Mowat's hands the compact theory was simply a tool to further local control of economic development. In Mercier's hands the compact theory was a legal justification for the notion that Quebec was completely sovereign within its own areas of jurisdiction — a sovereignty that would be used to guarantee Quebec's survival.

In 1888 Mercier's government passed the Jesuits' Estates Act, which provided some $400,000 of compensation to the Jesuit order for Jesuit property confiscated in 1773. Protestant extremists in Ontario were outraged that the government of a Canadian province could use public tax monies to support a religious order — dramatic evidence of the different perceptions of church-state relations in the two provinces. In fact, however, there was and is no formal, constitutional, separation of church and state in Canada, and Mercier was within his rights. Nevertheless, the French-English truce that had first broken down with the Riel hanging was dealt a further blow. The following year the Equal Rights Association made its appearance in Ontario and the West.

Although the Equal Rights Association has been much pilloried in the history books as little more than an anti-Catholic, anti-French rabble, it did put forward a view of Canada that was, in its own right, legitimate. Its major difficulty was that it could not possibly prevail in the Canada of the day. Led by a former Tory, D'Alton McCarthy, the ERA was opposed to state aid to separate (i.e., Catholic, in most cases) schools and to Catholic interference in politics. Its slogan was "equal rights for all, special privileges for none." Although it was most certainly rabidly anti-Catholic — and little different from extremist Protestant organizations such as the Orange Lodge in that regard — its desire to see a country where only individuals, and not groups, were endowed with rights was not inappropriate in a liberal-democratic society. It was inappropriate to the Canada of that day only because the existence of one particular group, endowed with its own special group rights, made the concept of "one person, one vote" quite impossible to introduce.

The ERA itself enjoyed almost no political success. Nevertheless, McCarthy's agitations in Manitoba were an important factor in prompting the Manitoba government to end tax support for Catholic schools in 1890 and virtually to eliminate the use of French in provincial institutions. Because Protestants outnumbered Catholics and few French Canadians had migrated to the West, such policies were easy enough to introduce. And they were another blow to French-English accommodation in Canada.

The Manitoba Schools Question, as historians call it, was the first overt attack by English-speaking Protestants on the right of Catholics — French or otherwise — to enjoy tax-supported schools. In the Manitoba case the attack was almost completely successful and, in the end, tax-supported Catholic schools disappeared from Manitoba. At almost the same time, French was eliminated as an admissible language of the courts and of other governmental institutions. Ottawa might have stepped in under the BNA Act to preserve tax support for Catholic schools, but neither the Tories nor the Liberals were anxious to do so. They feared alienating the Protestant majority both in Manitoba and in Ontario. Even Laurier (then still leader of the opposition) refused to take a hard line on the issue. He wanted to be prime minister, and offending English-speaking voters in Ontario would ruin his chances. Catholic rights in Manitoba seemed to him a cheap price to pay.

The Manitoba Schools Question dominated Canadian politics for much of the decade; it was followed by the North-West Schools Question in 1905. That issue centred on whether the new provinces of Saskatchewan and Alberta were to have separate schools. Laurier said yes; Clifford Sifton, Laurier's minister of immigration and unofficial western lieutenant, said no, and promptly resigned from the cabinet.

Unlike D'Alton McCarthy, Sifton was not an overt racist; but like McCarthy, he wanted a united Canada where immigrants would be assimilated into the Anglo-Saxon milieu as rapidly as possible. He was prepared to tolerate the French in Quebec, but he wanted to make it as difficult as possible for the French — or any other non-Anglo-Saxon people — to preserve their distinctiveness in the West. He believed, so to speak, in the melting-pot of British culture. As minister of immigration (he had joined the federal cabinet in 1896), he had done his best to bring immigrants to Canada from Eastern, Central, and Southern Europe. But he did so in the belief that sooner or later the significance of their distinctive origins would fade away. Thus he opposed separate schools, believing that a single system of public schools — he called them "national" schools — was a vital tool in the assimilative process. Sifton's views were consistent; prior to his entry into federal politics he had been a key member of the Manitoba government that had eliminated separate schools in that province. Laurier eventually watered down his proposals; and when the two new provinces were created, they did have a form of separate schooling.

The Manitoba and North-West Schools questions had arisen primarily because French Quebeckers had played virtually no role in the settlement of the West. Although Riel had secured French rights in Manitoba in 1870, almost no francophones came to Manitoba to exercise those rights. They did not want to wander far from home, hearth, and church. Despite their high birth rate, they preferred the familiar and the known to the unknown hardships of the prairie pioneering experience. Thus the existence of French (and Catholic) rights in the West hung by a tenuous thread. The English-speaking pioneers viewed the French language as just another exotic tongue, like Ukrainian, or German, or Finnish. It was, they thought, bound to disappear in the great process of assimilation and acculturation. Here was a major Canadian experience — the settlement of the West — that was not shared by Quebeckers.

The hanging of Riel, the Jesuits' Estates controversy, and the Manitoba Schools Question elicited two responses in Quebec. A small group took its cue from Jules-Paul Tardivel, a xenophobic, anti-Semitic nationalist who wished to create a conservative, Catholic republic on the banks of the St. Lawrence River. Here again was the Papineau tradition, although in a much more cramped version. Another Quebecker — Henri Bourassa — had a very different answer to the growing English-French crisis. He wanted Canada to become a single bicultural society, with French and English rights guaranteed in every corner of the nation, and he justified his dream by claiming that Canada had been established in the first place by "two founding peoples." Since "English" and "French" had created Canada, it followed that Canada should preserve the collective rights of both groups in all its national institutions.

When combined with the compact theory of Confederation,

Bourassa's vision of a country made of and by two peoples provided
much of the rationale behind the growth of Quebec nationalism
in the twentieth century and the widening gap between English-
speakers' and French-speakers' views of Canada. Since Canada
was formed by sovereign provinces, some Quebeckers reasoned,
Quebec was sovereign in its own right in those areas of jurisdiction reserved for it by the BNA Act. It was also the national
homeland of the French-Canadian people. By virtue of their status as a founding nation those people had prior rights not only
in Quebec, but in every corner of the land. Further, those rights
were above any other rights that might accrue to the immigrants
then arriving by their hundreds of thousands who were mostly
headed for western Canada. Those immigrants would be
required to assimilate, but the French would not. Bourassa stood
in opposition not only to Sifton, but also to generations of yet-
unborn westerners and the progeny of other immigrants who
have never understood why French-speaking Canadians could or
should enjoy special status across Canada. In effect, Bourassa was
resurrecting the concept of the "double majority" for Canada.
On some issues, the majority will of all Canadians would prevail;
but on others such as language rights, or the place of religious
institutions in society — in effect anything touching on the existence of the francophone community — there had to be agreement between two peoples, French and English. In other words,
a majority of each (thus a "double majority") would have to
agree or there would be no legitimacy to the decision. Such a
system of government can work only if there is clear and well-
defined agreement as to which decisions will be subject to majority rule and which to a double majority. That has never been the
case in Canada.

Bourassa and some of his followers had another objective, this
one specific to Quebec, that also helped shape the future of
Quebec's struggle for special status. Though a devout Catholic,
Bourassa realized that Quebec could not isolate itself from the
industrialization and urbanization that was transforming North
America and bringing non-French capitalists to Quebec's doors,

investment monies in hand. He and a small group of followers — intellectuals and journalists — urged the government of Quebec to bring Quebec into the twentieth century. They advocated nationalization of Quebec's natural resources, government ownership of the basic infrastructure, including hydro-electric-power generation, stimulation of investment in Quebec by French Quebeckers, and establishment of technical, vocational, and business schools. They believed that the key to survival was not to resist modernization, but to use the powers at the disposal of the provincial government to ensure that the urbanizing and industrializing processes had a distinctive French character and would be done primarily for the French community as a community.

Bourassa and Laurier were political rivals. Bourassa built much of his political career on the claim that Laurier could not be trusted to protect French interests; in fact, however, the two men were not far apart in their vision of Canada. The only real difference was that, as head of a national party, Laurier had political dues to pay outside Quebec and Bourassa did not. It was Laurier, after all, who wanted to see separate schools in Alberta and Saskatchewan; but more important, it was Laurier who spearheaded the fight against conscription during the First World War.

The fight for and against conscription in 1917 was not only a battle about military service, it was also a clash of visions of Canada. On one side stood Conservative prime minister Robert Laird Borden, supported by much of English-speaking Canada; on the other stood Laurier, champion of Quebec. Quebeckers had never warmed to this war. They saw it as an adventure in defending the British Empire, and they had never been enthusiastic about doing that — neither during the American Revolution nor in the War of 1812. They had grown even less inclined to defend British interests after the Riel affair, the schools issues, and all the other perceived attacks on their rights that had occurred since the mid-1880s. When Borden decided that Canada needed conscription to maintain manpower levels in its four divisions at the western front, Laurier led Quebec in bitter opposition. The battleground was the December 1917 federal election.

The 1917 election was one of the most bitterly contested electoral battles in Canadian history. Borden headed a coalition of Tories and English-speaking Liberals who deserted Laurier primarily because he was anticonscription. They charged that Laurier was aiding the enemy and that French Canadians were not much better than traitors because so few had volunteered for military service. Perhaps the best example of this thinking was that expressed by the otherwise liberal western newspaper editor, John W. Dafoe, in a letter to an old French-Canadian acquaintance: "French-Canadians have refused to play their part in this war — being the only known race of white men to quit. . . . Do not flatter yourself that the English Canadians are disturbed by your attitude of injured innocence or your threats of reprisal. . . . When we demonstrate, as we shall, that a solid Quebec is without power, there may be a return to reason along the banks of the St. Lawrence."

Borden, Dafoe, and their allies won, not surprisingly, and unleashed a torrent of anti-French feeling in the process. In Quebec the victory of the conscriptionists was viewed as a victory for oppression. French Canadians rioted in the streets. Troops were called out. Demonstrators were killed. Young French-Canadian males took to the hills to avoid the draft. The Tory party began its long political exile in Quebec. Papineau-style nationalism took hold in Quebec in the decades that followed. Dafoe had been right. Quebec was without power on those rare occasions when English-speaking Canada united against it. Not only did that realization rankle with French Canadians, it also reminded them of their minority status and of the dangers to which that status could expose them.

Many Canadians look to Canada's participation in the First World War as a turning point in Canada's march to nationhood. They point to Canada's achievements in that war, on both the battlefield and the home front, as evidence that Canada had become a nation. The Battle of Vimy Ridge, fought in April 1917, has long been celebrated as the very moment of that emergence. But the war was not nation-making because it was not a national experience. One major community — the French of Quebec — stayed as aloof as possible from the war. Although some French-Canadian males did volunteer for the armed forces — the famous Royal 22nd Regiment covered itself in glory — the level of participation was very low compared to that of the rest of Canada. Quebeckers neither wanted to share in the war experience nor understood the importance of the war to most of English-speaking Canada. On the other hand, English-speaking Canada did not understand the deep feeling of grievance that underlay much of Quebec's reluctance to become an enthusiastic partner in this national enterprise.

The conscription battle of 1917 was a turning point in Canadian history. The English-speaking majority had decided that it wished to fight the war to the greatest extent possible. It expected the French-speaking minority to respect that wish and to "do its duty" in the campaign. It viewed refusal to do so as treachery and a betrayal of the very liberty that the French minority had been granted as part of the Empire. The English-speaking majority was determined to go to virtually any length to impose its wishes on the French minority. It tolerated no dissent. It prevailed as it had done in 1885, and in 1890, showing again that it was not in sympathy with the Bourassa-Laurier "double majority" vision of Canada.

To the French minority, conscription meant one thing — that whenever the English-speaking majority decided it *must* win, it *would* win. To put it another way, the French minority had expected (or hoped) that some sort of double majority would determine the outcome of the conscription battle, but that had not happened. It was a bitter lesson, and it prompted a further turning inward among French Quebeckers. Now the Bourassa vision was given a new twist. The logic went like this. First, Ottawa was clearly the national government of English-speaking Canada. That had been proven by conscription. Second, it was an axiom that Canada had been founded by two peoples. Third, it was also an axiom that Quebec City was the national capital of French Canada. Fourth, it therefore followed that Quebec and Ottawa were the two poles in a bipolar relationship, with each holding sway in its own sphere.

These views emerged in Quebec between the wars in two forms: they were seized upon by a group of intellectuals and journalists led by cleric and historian Abbé Lionel Groulx, and they were championed by Premier Maurice Duplessis, who first came to power at the head of a provincial Union Nationale government in 1936. Groulx and his followers had a traditional Papineau-style answer to the travails of Quebec — outright independence and the formation of a clerically oriented republic on the banks of the St. Lawrence — "Laurentie," Groulx called it. If that was not immediately achievable, he favoured the isolation of Quebec within North America. This would be achieved by defending the old values of Catholicism, conservatism, and ruralism; by cutting Quebec off from the modernizing trends sweeping North America; by struggling against the tide of immigration and foreign capital investment that was already transforming Quebec; and by providing a comprehensive ideological framework to justify it all. The 1920s were the heyday of Catholic-oriented social action groups, many of which had been founded prior to the war. These church-sponsored organizations ministered to the needs of farmers, workers, youth, small investors and depositors, and so on. They mounted boycotts of Jewish-owned businesses and undertook to print daily fulminations against "foreigners," not only in the press but in ostensibly intellectual journals such as *Action française*, which Groulx founded in 1920. The result of all this activity was the further strengthening of insular French-Canadian nationalism and a nurturing of the already strong sense of grievance in the province.

As a major producer of primary products, Quebec was especially hard hit by the Great Depression. There, as in the rest of Canada, people demanded social and economic reform, guided by activist government, as the answer to their woes. But unlike the rest of Canada, Quebec couched its demands for reform in nationalist terms. It was not simply that "capitalism has failed," it was also that "the exploitative English have allowed French Quebec to descend into economic ruin." It did not take any great understanding of the economic system, for example, for the poverty-stricken French Catholic slum dwellers of the St. Henri district in Montreal to realize that the English-speaking élites who lived on the side of Mount Royal did not seem to be suffering very much. Thus what was, in many parts of North America, a nascent class struggle was, in Quebec, also a struggle of French against English. And in the popular mind, the government of Quebec had clearly thrown in its lot with the latter.

By the mid-1930s, therefore, Quebec politics was ripe for major transformation. The intellectuals and the tiny middle class were still ready to defend Catholic, conservative Quebec against the capitalist liberalism that held sway elsewhere in North America, while the poor, the working class, and the farmers were determined to wrest control of the province from their English-speaking oppressors. Virtually all groups in Quebec saw government activism as the answer to their problems. If the government of Quebec, the sole representative of the French collectivity, would seize the economic initiative, in much the same fashion as Bourassa and his followers had advocated at the turn of the century, Quebec as the homeland of the French community could be saved. Enter Maurice Duplessis.

Duplessis was elected in 1936 as part of a loose political alliance that brought together nationalist reformers who had broken with the corrupt provincial Liberal government (universally acknowledged to be in bed with the English-Canadian and American-owned companies that dominated the provincial economy) and provincial Conservatives. The coalition promulgated a platform of state-driven reforms designed to seize the reins of economic power from private capital and place them firmly in the hands of French Quebeckers. Duplessis, however, was an opportunist, not a reformer. He was interested in power, not change. And power flowed from English capital.

Soon after his election, Duplessis ditched his reform partners and ensconced himself as the virtual emperor of Quebec. For the people of Quebec he provided a flag — the blue and white fleur-de-lis. For the business leaders of Quebec he provided a deal — business as usual, *with* the power of the Quebec government to help keep down unruly unionists and persecute "communists" who dared to demand change. In exchange, he, his government, and his party would be taken care of. For the Groulx-nurtured intellectuals and church leaders Duplessis provided a vision — fortress Quebec. Against Ottawa's scheming, interventionist initiatives his provincial government would use the word *non* as often as necessary to ensure that Quebeckers alone (conveniently maintaining a discreet silence regarding his corporate allies) determined Quebec's future. This was Duplessis's version of "defending Quebec's autonomy," and although it was, in many respects, inconsistent and even farcical, it did continue the tradition that the government of Quebec was the prime defender of the *survivance* of the French-Canadian heartland. Once again, Papineau's spirit found a home in Quebec City.

Duplessis would probably have remained in power for twenty-three unbroken years until his death in 1959 if it hadn't been for his only real political mistake: in October 1939 he called a provincial election and threw the gauntlet down to the federal government, headed by Liberal William Lyon Mackenzie King. He challenged Ottawa's right to use wartime emergency powers to direct the national war effort. He was trounced by the provincial Liberal Party. But that happened only because King's Quebec ministers intervened directly in the election and threatened to resign if Duplessis won. Since King had pledged to Quebec that there would be no conscription, Quebeckers were asked to decide who would best protect their interests in wartime — the Liberal ministers in Ottawa or the Union Nationale government in Quebec City. King won and, for a brief moment, the spirit of LaFontaine reigned supreme in Quebec politics.

That all ended in 1942. It was one thing for King to declare that there would be no conscription at the outbreak of war — King feared that conscription would tear the national fabric as surely as it had done in 1917; it was another to keep that pledge as Allied disaster followed Allied disaster. By early 1942 the Japanese controlled southeast Asia and much of the Pacific, the Nazis were deep inside the U.S.S.R., and France had long been knocked out of the war. English-speaking Canada wanted full participation in the war, with no holding back of manpower or resources. The demand for conscription grew, and King was forced to give ground. His plan was to outflank his opponents by calling a national plebiscite to seek release from his "no conscription" pledge. The vote was held in April 1942. Led by the Ligue pour la défense du Canada, a French-Canadian nationalist movement that included the likes of Pierre Elliott Trudeau, 72.9 per cent of Quebeckers voted *non*. But in English-speaking Canada the result was almost exactly the opposite. King was released from his pledge and, in November 1944, after delaying as long as possible, he agreed to bring in conscription.

The conscription crisis of 1942-44 was not as damaging to national unity as that of 1917 had been. Unlike Borden in 1917, King had fought valiantly against the measure, and he was clearly forgiven by most Quebeckers. His senior French ministers, including Louis St. Laurent who had been drafted from a successful Quebec City law practice to be King's Quebec lieutenant in December 1941, stayed with the government. And the Liberal Party of Canada captured fifty-four out of sixty-five seats in Quebec in the 1945 federal election. But conscription did open the door to Duplessis once again. He swept back into power in Quebec City in 1944.

Canada's participation in the Second World War was another glaring example of a so-called national enterprise that was, in fact, not at all national. Perhaps 100,000 French Canadians volunteered for military service, a fraction of those who were eligible. Once again, there was little sympathy for, or understanding of, the issues that lay behind the war. And although there was lit-

tle support for Hitler in Quebec, there was considerable endorse-
ment for the pro-Nazi Vichy regime established in the south of
France following the French surrender to the Germans in the
spring of 1940. Many leading Quebec intellectuals, clergymen,
and journalists saw Vichy as a welcome counterbalance to what
they claimed was the Jewish-led, communist/socialist-dominated
republic it replaced. Indeed, the principles that the Vichy government espoused — "Travail, Famille, Patrie" (work, family,
homeland); as opposed to the "Liberty, Equality, Fraternity" of
the French Republic — were not much different from the objectives pursued by generations of Quebec leaders. Had it not been
for Quebec, Canada would undoubtedly have introduced conscription soon after the start of the war, and the war would have
been a genuine nation-building experience.

The war changed Canada and it changed Quebec. Canada
emerged as a more industrialized, more urbanized, more tech-
nologically advanced society than it had been in 1939. After the
war, hundreds of thousands of veterans attended universities,
colleges, and technical and vocational schools under federal veterans' programs and became better educated and able to command better wages and salaries in the process. A large middle
class emerged for the first time to play a major role in Canadian
politics. The labour movement gained the right to collective bargaining and grew into a permanent and powerful force in politics and the economy. Within three years after the war the federal government took the momentous step of deliberately opening
Canada's doors to hundreds of thousands of European war
refugees in an effort to expand Canada's population base. At the
same time, the King government created the beginnings of a
welfare state by using the tremendous economic and fiscal powers available to it under the Constitution. For the first time, the
government not only attempted to regulate the ebb and flow of
economic life, but also introduced family allowances, veterans'
benefits, government control of mortgage interest rates, price
supports for farm products, and so on. As we noted earlier, there

were two major reasons behind this growth in government interventionism: first, Canadians and their leaders feared the re-
emergence of the Great Depression after the war and demanded
government action to stop this from happening; and second,
Canadians came to believe that the government should do in
peacetime what it had done so effectively in war — regulate life
to a much greater degree in the interests of what they took to be
the common good. In Ottawa, as we saw in chapter one, a group
of bureaucrats had emerged into positions of authority who
strongly believed that the federal government had a legitimate
role to play in regulating capitalism so as to provide full employment and a more equal distribution of wealth than had previously existed.

In order to accomplish even greater objectives — such as the
introduction of a national health-insurance program — Ottawa
needed provincial co-operation either to change the Constitution or to make financial agreements under the existing Constitution that would allow the federal government to provide more
services but also to collect more tax monies. The initial federal
proposals were put to the provinces at a marathon federal-
provincial conference that opened in August 1945 and lasted
(on and off) for the better part of a year. Ontario, led by Tory
premier George Drew, was strongly opposed to such action;
Duplessis was not far behind. The old Ontario-Quebec alliance,
initially formed in the days of Oliver Mowat and Honoré Mercier, re-emerged. The federal government was stopped dead in its
tracks; the conference ended in April 1946 with nothing accomplished. Medicare, among other things, had been stymied, and
Drew and Duplessis were still lords of their own domains.

The failure of the 1945-46 federal-provincial conference was
one factor that brought about King's retirement two years later.
The man who had led Canada (with two Tory interregnums, one
of only three months) since the end of 1921 was old, tired, and
less and less in control of events. At the federal Liberal leadership convention in August 1948, St. Laurent succeeded him. St.
Laurent was very much in the Laurier tradition. He was perfectly

bilingual, having grown up speaking French to his father and English to his mother. (In later life he recalled his shock at being able to speak French to the mother of one of his friends!) At the same time, he was fiscally conservative, and he strongly believed in the need for Quebec to play an active role in federal politics through the Liberal Party; he was a liberal-democrat who abhorred Duplessis's authoritarian ways. "Uncle Louis" was also very popular both in Quebec and in English-speaking Canada and led his party to landslide victories in the federal elections of 1949 and 1953. Once again Quebeckers had the best of both worlds — a Papineau in Quebec City and a LaFontaine in Ottawa.

Although Ontario under Drew and Quebec under Duplessis appeared to be acting together in the late 1940s, there was a major difference in the motivations of the two men. Drew wanted to enhance the power of Ontario in Confederation both out of traditional political ambition and in the belief that the government of Ontario, being "closer" to the people, was better able to minister to their needs. That was also true of Duplessis, except that a third factor always motivated Quebec's leaders. If the power of the federal government was enhanced, the authority of the only true government of the French-Canadian people, one that they controlled and the only one (Duplessis would have claimed) that existed solely to protect their interests and work primarily for their *survivance* would necessarily be diminished. That could never be allowed to happen. Thus for Quebec, power could flow only outward from Ottawa, never inward. What was ironic about this, however, is that Duplessis had no plans to use even the very ample powers that his government already had under the constitution, let alone any new ones wrested from Ottawa.

Duplessis responded to the changing times by opposing the welfare state, by trying to block federal initiatives, by refusing to participate in federally initiated shared-cost programs, and by refusing to take federal cash for universities, hospitals, and

social-welfare institutions. Quebec's social and educational programs remained as they had been since the turn of the century.
While the rest of North America moved rapidly into the second
half of the twentieth century, Duplessis's Quebec, on the surface, remained a conservative, pious, priest-ridden society, open
(on Duplessis's terms) to foreign capital, but closed to social
justice.

Underneath the surface, it was another matter. Quebec was
changing, and Duplessis was no more successful in stopping the
transformation than King Canute had been in stopping the
incoming tide. Quebec too became even more urbanized and
industrialized. Tens of thousands of its veterans also went to universities, colleges, and vocational and training schools under veterans' training programs. A middle class grew there too, and
society became more stable, wealthier, and more North American than ever. And although intellectuals, journalists, artists, and
the handful of native Quebec business leaders were certainly
nationalists in that they wanted French Canada to preserve itself,
they most decidedly did not share Duplessis's cramped, conservative, authoritarian view of the world. They wanted two related
goals: (1) the transformation of Quebec into a modern,
advanced, liberal-democratic society, free of the social and political domination of the Catholic church; and (2) the preservation
of Quebec's French culture and identity.

One other objective also determined their future direction.
The newly emerging middle and managerial classes were frustrated by a system that gave them the educational skills necessary
to move to the top but denied them promotion above middle-
management levels because they were francophones. In the one
province where they were in a decided majority, it was the
English-speakers, not they, who held the levers of economic
power, who earned the top dollars, who occupied the executive
suites. This too would have to change.

Any astute observer examining the state of Canada in the
early 1950s would have seen some disturbing signs that all was
not right within this unique dominion that, according to popu-

lar myth, had brought two disparate peoples together in one society. For one thing, Quebeckers clearly believed that their government was something more than another provincial government — it was the guardian of Quebec's nationality. That would bode ill for the future of Canadian federalism as soon as someone succeeded Duplessis who was determined to use the powers of the Quebec government to ensure French survival in the way that Henri Bourassa had first suggested. For another, Quebec was no more a part of the national fabric in 1957 than it had been in 1867, despite nine decades of shared experience. In some ways, it was less a part of Canada. What should have been the great national experiences of ending the economic disaster of the 1930s and fighting a victorious war had, in fact, driven Quebec farther into isolation.

As long as Duplessis reigned, he could be dismissed in English-speaking Canada, and by federal politicians, as a power-hungry quasi dictator, feeding his megalomania and representing little more than himself and his corrupt cronies. The deep divisions in Canada that existed below the surface could be ignored. It was easy to believe that there was nothing fundamentally wrong with the country. But all that changed on the night of June 22, 1960. After that Canada would never again be the same, sane, place it had once seemed to be.

3

THE HEADWATERS OF MEECH LAKE

n the early morning hours of June 3, 1987, Prime Minister Brian Mulroney and Canada's ten provincial premiers emerged from the inner sanctums of the Langevin Building, on the south side of Wellington Street across from Parliament Hill, to announce that they had reached agreement on the final text of the Meech Lake Accord. The eleven men had been holed up for almost twenty hours. They had come to Ottawa to put the final touches on a package of constitutional proposals designed, as Mulroney put it, to "bring Quebec into the family." The Meech Lake Accord had originally been hammered out at the end of April in another marathon bargaining session held at the federal government's retreat at Meech Lake, just north of Ottawa. It was designed to secure Quebec's formal assent to the Constitution Act of 1982.

The Meech Lake Accord proposed radical changes to the nature of Canada. Among other things, it would have reduced the national government to the status of first among equals, crippled its ability to carry out its historic and necessary mission of setting Canada's national agenda, and slammed the door on any future moves to Senate reform. But the most radical changes would have occurred as a result of this clause:

> 2. (1) The Constitution of Canada shall be interpreted in a manner consistent with (a) the recognition that the existence of French-speaking Canadians, centred in Quebec but also present elsewhere in Canada, and English-speaking Canadians, concentrated outside Quebec but also present in Quebec, constitutes a fundamental characteristic of Canada; and (b) the recognition that Quebec constitutes within Canada a distinct society.
>
> (2) The role of the Parliament of Canada and the provincial legislatures to preserve the fundamental characteristic of Canada referred to in paragraph (1)(a) is affirmed.
>
> (3) The role of the legislature and government of Quebec to preserve and promote the distinct identity of Quebec referred to in (1)(b) is affirmed.

This clause, which endowed the government of Quebec with special legal and constitutional responsibilities, was utterly unprecedented in Canadian history. It would have given to Quebec alone the authority to "promote and preserve" Quebec's distinctiveness — a clear victory-from-the-grave for Papineau. It would have set the stage for a significant expansion of the powers of the Quebec government, allowing it to act and legislate in fields not open to the legislatures of the other provinces. It would, in short, have created two classes of Canadians — those in Quebec and those outside it. Whatever the implications for Canadian federalism, it served to undermine completely one of the fundamental pillars of liberal democracy: equality of all citizens before the law.

The Meech Lake Accord would have been the penultimate blow to Canada as a nation. It was bad enough to confer special status on Quebec; but that concession would not have been enough for Quebec's ambitious nationalist leaders. They were united on at least one thing during the Meech Lake debate — Quebec's demands at Meech Lake represented *minimums*, the *least* that Quebec was prepared to accept. The dynamic of events,

as they have unfolded since 1960, would undoubtedly have led
to a period in which Quebec tested its new powers and, when it
inevitably found that these were not enough, to a demand for
more. Since the Meech Lake agreement came about primarily
because Prime Minister Mulroney succeeded in bribing the leaders of the other nine provinces with powers and status almost
equal to those granted to Quebec, each step Quebec took
towards separation would have been matched, though probably
not to as extreme a degree, by the other provinces. Whether or
not Quebec would have finally separated, Canada would have
lost its soul. With its national government denuded of power, its
provincial leaders enthroned as mini-potentates, and its will or
ability to choose national courses of action severely handi-
capped, if not destroyed, Canada might have continued to exist
on the map, but as little more than a name, an excuse for retaining a flag and an anthem (actually, two very different anthems
with the same tune) and for fielding a hockey team.

In signing the Meech Lake Accord, Canada's eleven first ministers were accepting, holus-bolus: (1) the Mowat-Mercier fantasy
that Canada was created by the provinces; (2) Henri Bourassa's
fiction that Canada was a compact of two founding language
groups; (3) Maurice Duplessis's corollary that Ottawa and Quebec were co-equal, each the government of one of Canada's
major linguistic groups; and (4) the demand made by former
Quebec premiers Jean Lesage (1960-66) and Daniel Johnson
(1966-68) that Quebec had (or ought to have) a legal and constitutional special status in Confederation. These leaders were, at
the same time, rejecting the view held by every Canadian prime
minister from Macdonald to Trudeau that, although Quebec was
clearly and obviously distinct in that the majority of its people
are French, it must not and could not have a special legal or
constitutional status within Confederation. How was it that the
grandiose dreams of generations of Quebec political thinkers
had come to be accepted by the men (they were all men) at the
very centre of political power in Canada? How was it that the distorted view of Canada represented by the Meech Lake Accord

became, in the spring of 1987, the accepted conventional wisdom of the Canadian political mainstream? Thereby hangs our tale.

On the night of June 22, 1960, the Quebec Liberal Party under former federal cabinet minister Jean Lesage was elected to govern Quebec. It was not an overwhelming victory; Lesage's party won fifty-one seats to the Union Nationale's forty-three. Duplessis's death in 1959 had ushered in a brief but frenetic period of self-examination and reform within the ranks of the Union Nationale that helped its cause in the election, but it was too little too late. Lesage's Liberals — a coalition of old-style provincial Liberals who had wandered in the wilderness since the Second World War and young, vigorous, nationalist reformers — were handed the task of bringing Quebec's governmental, social, and economic institutions into the twentieth century. Within a few days it was apparent to all observers that a new era had dawned. Lesage appointed a cabinet in which activists were prominent. Some, like René Lévesque, were new to politics but had been important in the rising tide of social and political reform that had emerged in Quebec even before Duplessis's death. Lévesque had been a political commentator and reporter on the French CBC network and had led a strike of French producers against the CBC in Montreal in 1959 that had been sparked by a CBC threat to curtail French-language news programming.

The new government's first moves were more symbolic than substantial. It was announced that all government contracts would henceforth be let through the public-tendering process. A veteran of the Royal Canadian Mounted Police was installed as boss of the corrupt Quebec Provincial Police (which had often acted as Duplessis's private army) with instructions to clean house. A prominent judge known for his toughness and incorruptibility was appointed head of the Quebec Liquor Commission, which had been one of the Union Nationale's most important milch cows. Talks were begun with Ottawa to gain access to federal funds for hospital insurance and for construction of the

Quebec portion of the Trans-Canada Highway. It was a heady time. It was "thirty days that shook the province," in the words of *Le Devoir*. It was a "quiet revolution" in the opinion of the *Globe and Mail*. The phrase caught on.

The initial objectives of this Quiet Revolution were traditional: to issue a strong signal that the corruption of the Duplessis period was over; to tell the world that the Liberals would operate in an open, democratic fashion; to proclaim that the insularity that had marked Duplessis's relationships with Ottawa was a thing of the past. Ottawa had earmarked funds for this or that and Duplessis had, for the most part, refused to accept the largesse; Quebec would now seek its fair share. Did that mean that Quebec was prepared to become a province like the others, sitting as an equal at the table with the other provinces and accepting federal leadership in the introduction of new measures? Far from it.

How was the Quiet Revolution revolutionary? It was certainly not revolutionary in its battle against corruption, commendable as that was. Governments battle corruption all the time. Nor was it revolutionary in its basic view about Quebec's place in Canada or in its belief that the prime role of the government of Quebec was to ensure *la survivance*. Not surprisingly, the Lesage government shared all the assumptions about these matters that had been held by Duplessis and his predecessors stretching back at least as far as Mercier: Quebec was the only homeland of the francophone minority in Canada; the Quebec government had a sacred duty to use the powers it possessed to achieve its objective of protecting the interests of that minority; the Quebec government spoke for the francophone community while Ottawa represented "English Canada"; Canada had been founded by "two founding peoples" and was a compact between those peoples as well as a compact of the provinces.

Much of the foundation for the Lesage government's constitutional position had been laid by a Quebec royal commission established by the Duplessis government in 1953. The Royal

Commission of Inquiry on Constitutional Problems, chaired by
Judge Thomas Tremblay, was established by an act of the Quebec legislature in February 1953. It was charged with formulat-
ing Quebec's response to the increased activism of the federal
government since the end of the Second World War, not only in
the spheres of fiscal, economic, and social policy, but also in the
area of cultural policy. This last was apparent from some of the
recommendations that the federal Royal Commission on National Development in the Arts, Letters and Sciences — the Massey
Commission — had issued in its 1951 report. Operating on the
assumption that Canada had a national culture and that the federal government should play an active role in promoting that
culture in all its facets (including higher education, scientific
research, and the arts) the Massey Commission had recommended the creation of a federally funded agency — the Canada
Council — to oversee and guide federal involvement in the promotion and direction of Canadian culture. In Quebec this was
viewed as a dangerous intrusion into Quebec affairs. "English"
Canada might have its own culture, and the federal government
might have a role to play in promoting it, but only Quebec City
had a role to play in the preservation and promotion of French
culture!

The very legislation creating the Tremblay Commission tells
much about what it was charged to do. It reiterated the notion
that Canada was a cultural compact between two founding peoples — Henri Bourassa's old *canard* — and that those two peoples shared equal rights and privileges. The government of Quebec was also proclaimed to represent the French community, the
government of Canada the English community. It asserted that
in order to carry out its mission of protecting the interests of
one of Canada's two, co-equal, founding communities, the government of Quebec needed to have the fiscal resources to preserve its financial independence. It was the commission's mission to suggest ways to do this, not to discuss, question, or justify
the assumptions that governed its mandate.

Duplessis undoubtedly expected the commissioners to present him with precisely those arguments he needed in his battles with Ottawa, and nothing more. He was half correct. The commission actually conducted an extensive, wide-ranging study of Canadian constitutional history from a by-then traditional Quebec perspective, the history of the French communities both inside and outside Quebec, and Canada's current fiscal arrangements and the distribution of powers between Ottawa and the provinces. The commission's basic operating assumptions were those developed by Mercier, Bourassa, Groulx, and other Quebec leaders — mostly in the Papineau tradition. It also took careful note of the bitter experiences of lost battles over Manitoba schools and conscription. Its primary recommendations were that the government of Quebec should be far more active in guiding not only the cultural life of the province, but also its economic, social, and industrial development. In the words of political scientist William Coleman the commission believed that: "The government of Quebec had to receive sufficient powers to enable it to act as the national government of the French-Canadian nation. These powers included sole responsibility for education, for the delivery of social services, for the support of culture, and even for the deployment of natural resources." It followed naturally that Quebec should, at the very least, move fully into the field of direct taxation — which Duplessis did by introducing a Quebec income tax in early 1954.

In some ways the recommendations of the Tremblay Commission were stillborn. For one thing, Duplessis was not about to change his philosophy of government at that point in his career. For another, again in the words of Professor Coleman, "the revolution called for by the Tremblay Commission never took place because the values it cherished were jettisoned." Those values, not surprisingly given the commission's membership — one was a disciple of Groulx, another a specialist in Catholic social thought, while Tremblay himself was a friend and confidant of Duplessis — were the traditional Catholic ones that were already being eroded within the hearts and minds of the intelligentsia, within the new middle class, as well as among the province's labour leaders.

Although the Tremblay Commission had little immediate impact on the government of Quebec, it helped focus the thinking of many Quebeckers not so much on how to preserve a Catholic, conservative Quebec, but on what the desired role of the Quebec government should be in the post-war world. It was here that the Lesage government came up with its revolutionary answer. It would push forward in every constitutional field available to it to test the limits of its powers and to see what it could achieve with those powers. It would attempt to carve away from the federal government areas of jurisdiction that, according to its reading of constitutional history, ought to belong to it; and it would work within those areas to advance the interests of the French community. Like the Duplessis government before it, Lesage's government would challenge Ottawa's right to legislate, even to provide leadership in, shared-cost programs such as hospital insurance (and, later, medicare among others). Unlike the Duplessis government, however, it would not refuse to participate in those programs and let Ottawa bank the funds earmarked for Quebec. It would, instead, insist on its right to set up its own parallel programs with those earmarked funds. All this flowed from the deeply held belief that Quebec was not a province like the others but had a different, national, mission to fulfil. Thus the Quebec government would fill the role once occupied by the Catholic church, a role that even by 1960 had been more and more abandoned in an increasingly secularized society. The new church was the government of Quebec, the new religion was French nationalism, the new clergy were the political leaders, intellectuals, and bureaucrats who would serve the needs of "the parishioners" who were the people of French Quebec. This was communalism raised to a high art.

Did Quebec need the additional powers it sought, then, under Lesage, and seeks now, in the post-Meech era? It is time to consider this question, because it lies at the heart of the current constitutional crisis. The question was mooted by the Tremblay Commission but, for the most part, the answer was never pursued by Duplessis. It was then placed front and centre by the Lesage Liberals and became the basis for Quebec's constitutional demands under every government since. Not surprisingly the answer provided by those governments was always yes. (What political leader ever campaigns for diminished power?) And it has become sacred scripture, taken as gospel truth even by many people in English-speaking Canada, that yes is indeed the correct answer. This is a prime example of the old saw that if something is repeated often enough, it must be true.

In order for it to be true, however, several other assumptions would also have to be true. First, the government of Quebec would have to be the only government charged with preserving the French community. Second, the government of Quebec would have to be the only government capable of preserving the French community. Neither assumption is self-evidently valid; both have been questioned from the time of LaFontaine to the era of Pierre Trudeau.

By 1960 Canada was already a highly decentralized country, notwithstanding the federal initiatives taken since 1945 in social, economic, fiscal, and cultural areas. For example, inside the so-called economic union that Canada is supposed to be there existed (and still exist) many formidable barriers to interprovincial trade. In addition, the federal government had no direct jurisdiction over social policy, no jurisdiction over labour relations within each province, no jurisdiction over transportation or communications within each province, unless it could be demonstrably shown to the courts that the transportation or communications matter in question was clearly national in scope and/or impact. Ottawa had jurisdiction over interprovincial trade, but that jurisdiction had been only narrowly interpreted by the courts. Virtually all the measures Ottawa had devised to fight the Great Depression in the 1930s had been struck down by the courts, all the measures it had used to organize Canada for war in 1914-18 and 1939-45 had been dissolved once the wars were over. Each of the provinces had (and has) sole control over its education and labour relations, the development of internal

communications including intraprovincial railways and high-
ways, the exploitation of natural resources, the establishment of
barriers to trade (such as exclusionary regulations barring products and services from other provinces). Ottawa had (and has)
broader taxing powers than the provinces, but each province
had the power to levy a wide variety of direct taxes including
income and corporate taxes, sales taxes, and death duties. And
although there was no amending formula to change the Canadian Constitution — it was, until 1982, a statute of the British Parliament and could be changed only by that parliament — there
was an unwritten assumption that all the provinces had to agree
before the BNA Act could be changed. The government of
Canada thus had considerably less power in relation to the
provinces than the government of the United States did in relation to the states.

From the very first interprovincial get-together in 1887 — the
Interprovincial Conference called by Mowat and hosted by
Mercier — the provinces have tried to improve on their position
vis-à-vis Ottawa. They sought more powers from Ottawa. They
tried to stop Ottawa from expanding its sphere of powers. They
challenged Ottawa in the courts whenever new matters not
referred to in the BNA Act — such as broadcasting or aviation
— arose. Quebec played its part in this, but until 1960, the leading role in the attack on Ottawa was more often played by
Ontario. Ontario defended its existing powers and sought new
ones not because it saw itself as playing a special role as the
prime government responsible for protecting English-speaking
Canada but because of the vanity or ambition of its leaders,
because of the role given it in the federation of protecting the
interests of Ontarians against those of Canadians living in other
provinces, because of its size and wealth. That give and take
between governments that share sovereignty (the national government is sovereign in its areas of power, the provinces within
theirs) is the creative dissonance inherent in any federal system.

What, then, were Quebec's motives? Was it involved in the
struggle to enhance its authority for the same reasons that moti-

vated Ontario? Was it, then, acting just like any other province (even while proclaiming that it was not like the others) in trying to get more power? That was certainly true up to 1960. But after that date, it began to claim powers not equal but greater than Ontario's. Were these really and truly needed to preserve Quebec's distinct culture, or were Quebec's political leaders just using cultural arguments to get what most politicians (in Quebec, Ontario, or Timbuktu) want — more power in general?

Whatever the "true" answer to the question "Did/does Quebec truly need powers additional to those possessed by the other provinces?" the history of Quebec under the Lesage and subsequent governments leads us to believe that it did not need them. The two most important steps taken by the Lesage government in the early 1960s were both taken within the existing Constitution. These were the nationalization of Quebec's private power companies and the creation of the Quebec Pension Plan (QPP) and the Caisse de dépôt et placement du Québec, which is the repository of the QPP funds.

The initiative for the nationalization of the private power companies was taken by René Lévesque. As minister of hydraulic resources in 1962, Lévesque began to push hard for the measure both within cabinet and in reformist circles within the party. Reformers viewed this as a key element in the drive of Quebeckers to become *maîtres chez nous* — masters in our own house. It had been advocated by Henri Bourassa and his followers as far back as the turn of the century and was one of the unfulfilled pledges made by Duplessis when he was first elected in 1936.

In 1944 the Liberal government of Joseph-Adélard Godbout had nationalized the Montreal Light, Heat and Power Consolidated company to create Hydro-Québec, a small company with operations limited to the Montreal area. It paled in comparison to Ontario Hydro, the government-owned electric power monopoly that had kept generation and distribution costs low in Ontario since the turn of the century. That had been good for individual consumers and a boon to the province's industry.

Lévesque and his supporters now wanted to expand Hydro-Québec into a province-wide monopoly, both to give the Quebec government a strategic instrument and to stop the outflow of profits to English-speaking Canadian and American shareholders. It was going to be prohibitively expensive; the cost would be approximately $400 million, which was about the same as some recent provincial budgets. After a thorough discussion and debate within the cabinet, Lévesque prevailed and Lesage decided to go to the people of Quebec to seek a mandate specifically on this issue. On November 14, 1962, the Liberals won their second straight election with 56.5 per cent of the popular vote. Within eight months the buy-out of the private power companies had been completed.

The transformation of Hydro-Québec into a government-owned monopoly was one of the most important milestones along Quebec's road to self-determination. At one stroke a giant tool was created that could regulate and exploit the bounteous water resources of the province. The massive James Bay Project embarked upon in 1971 would not have been possible without this move. That project has turned Quebec into a major source of electrical power for the northeastern United States. At present Quebec is embarking on James Bay II, another major power development that could underpin the economy of an independent Quebec. This too flows from the take-over of the private power companies some thirty years ago. That nationalization was possible because Quebec, like the other provinces, has total control over property and civil rights in the province under the current Constitution. It needed no extra powers either to carry out the nationalization or to exploit the water-power resources of the province, in 1971 or now.

Nor did Quebec need extra powers to launch its own pension plan, a move undertaken following a short but sharp battle with the Liberal government of Lester B. Pearson in late 1963 and early 1964. That battle was joined following the Pearson minority election victory of April 22, 1963, when Ottawa announced that it would introduce a national contributory pension plan.

The Canada Pension Plan was to be a cornerstone of the Pearson government's reform program.

The Lesage government refused to participate in Ottawa's scheme. Judy LaMarsh, Canada's minister of national health and welfare, thought Quebec merely wanted to ensure that the Canada Pension Plan was translated into French. In fact, however, the brilliant bureaucrats at Quebec City had already figured out that a pension plan under their own control would create a major capital pool out of the contributions of employers and employees and that the capital from this pool could be strategically invested for the benefit of Quebeckers.

The issue came to a head at a federal-provincial conference held in Quebec City in late March and early April 1964. There Lesage unveiled his own plans for a Quebec pension plan that was better than the federal plan in almost every way. Ottawa was forced to give ground. In meetings held after the conference it both adopted many of the features of the Quebec plan and conceded that any province had a right to introduce a plan of its own. None did, of course, because Quebec's objectives were not merely financial, they were also psychological. As Jean Lesage told the Quebec legislature: "I have worked for my province as no man has ever worked for it. I have made use of all the means which Providence granted . . . so that Quebec, finally, could be recognized as a province which has a *statut spécial* (special status) in Confederation." The total value of the Caisse de dépôt et de placement, which holds the QPP funds, is currently approaching $40 billion. It is the largest pool of capital in Canada. It has consistently been used, and will continue to be used, as a source of strategic investment capital upon which Quebec entrepreneurs may continually draw. Much of the economic activity that the French point to as evidence of their new managerial and entrepreneurial prowess has been financed by this state source of funds. It too was created without the need for special additional powers.

It is thus demonstrably plain that Quebec, under Lesage and

subsequent governments, has had strong levers of power — financial, economic, and cultural — *under current constitutional arrangements* to ensure not only *la survivance* but also *l'épanouissement* — the flourishing of its culture. Why then has it sought special powers and special guarantees through all the endless rounds of constitutional wrangling that have taken place virtually without end since the early 1960s? Why did it hold, unbending, to its position in the Meech Lake round? Why is it seeking even more now?

Before we give our answer to this question, we want to make it abundantly clear that there is one area where Quebec was and is, we believe, fully entitled to special status of a kind within Canada. As the home of North America's only significant francophone community, Quebec is entitled to a veto over any constitutional arrangements that would endanger the status of the French language in Quebec as long as that veto is fully consistent with the basic principles of Canadian nationhood. Thus it was and is reasonable for Quebec to possess powers that would protect it from suffering the sort of attack on its right to preserve its language that the francophone community of Manitoba suffered in the fight over separate schools there. Given historical developments and political realities, we believe that Quebec is reasonable in trying to ensure that its ability to protect the francophone community in Quebec is not diminished by the actions of others. Unfortunately, that is not all that Quebec seeks.

Since the Quiet Revolution, Quebec's definitions of "language" and "culture" and the threats thereto have been so broad and so loose that they have resulted in demands for a broad range of additional powers that threaten the very existence of Canada. We believe that the powers Quebec claims it needs to protect its French culture are not needed, and were never needed. An examination of the vibrancy; the dynamism; the innovativeness; the cultural, economic, entrepreneurial, educational, and social advances made by Quebeckers since the Quiet Revolution — made with powers no greater than those of Ontario or any other province and with no significant changes to the balance of federal and provincial powers — proves that point. We believe that Quebec's leaders want more powers not because they are needed, but because, swallowing those notions enunciated by Papineau, Mercier, Henri Bourassa, Groulx, and Duplessis, Quebec's leaders, supported by its journalists, intellectuals, and artists, have also swallowed the idea that a "state" such as Quebec, ought to have those powers and is entitled to them simply because they declare it to be so!

To put this another way, Quebec is not seeking more powers in order to provide a more effective provincial administration for its people. It is not attempting, as is Alberta, or British Columbia, or New Brunswick, to be somehow more effective in advancing the provincial/regional interests of its residents. Instead, Quebec is seeking those fiscal, legislative, and economic powers consistent with the vision it has developed of itself over the past century: the vision of a *nation state* within Canada, the heartland of one of Canada's two founding peoples whose consent made Canada possible!

Does this mean that Lesage was a "separatist" who secretly sought independence? No; and his campaigning for the *non* side in the 1980 referendum on sovereignty-association is proof enough of that. For Lesage, and for all his so-called federalist successors, "special status" was, quite simply, statehood without the pain and with few of the costs of real statehood. Why discuss separation at all, he often proclaimed as premier, when Quebec had not yet tested the full range of its powers within Confederation? Why indeed!

Lesage, a man of great integrity, thought of separation as a goal, not as a threat. His successor, Union Nationale premier Daniel Johnson, thought differently. His theme was *"égalité ou indépendance"* — equality for Quebec or independence. He did not mean by that "equality with the other provinces," he meant equality with Ottawa. His expectation was that equality was not far off. He no doubt thought it would be more quickly achieved under the threat of separation. Thus for him separation was a threat, not a goal.

The roots of this sort of thinking can be traced back to Confederation itself, but the campaign to achieve a special status in law to match the special status Quebec has always had in the hearts and minds of Quebec's leaders accelerated after 1960. It paralleled and was not unconnected to the re-emergence during the 1960s of separatism in Quebec. There were several major reasons for this. In part the separatist movement was rooted in Quebec's own sense of historical grievance. In part it was linked to the achievement of independence by third-world nations during the 'sixties. Much of the early and rather crude rhetoric of separatism in Quebec amounted to little more than self-conscious parroting of the Marxist, anti-American, anticolonialist gospel as preached in various Asian and African capitals. Some of the separatist sentiment was also connected to the yearnings of Quebec journalists, authors, artists, and other political dilettantes for a country of their own, complete with a U.N. seat and a national anthem, wherein they would not have to make compromises with *les anglais*. In the atmosphere of freedom and experimentation unloosed by the Quiet Revolution, these sentiments began to lay claim to the hearts of many French Quebeckers, René Lévesque not least among them. Thus Lesage and his successors had to perform a balancing act between the reality that independence could be a disaster for Quebec and the dreams of the writers, artists, and intellectuals who yearned for Quebec's "liberty." They knew full well that a Canada that had, for the most part, allowed Quebec to be ensconced at the centre of power from the very start had been a very good thing for Quebec. They might even have totted up Quebec's losses (Manitoba Schools, conscription, etc.) and realized that they were far fewer than Quebec's gains. The compromise they arrived at, then and now, was to try to define a "special status" for Quebec — a status befitting Quebec's "statehood" — within Canada. The difficulty was in getting the rest of Canada to buy the notion.

Given the changes that had taken place in Quebec society since the end of the Second World War, it is not surprising that a great

deal of nationalism and national pride emerged. The most important change was the decline in the secular influence of the church
and in the very religiosity of the people of Quebec. For a variety of
complex and interrelated reasons, most of which stemmed from
the growth of an educated middle class, Catholicism ceased to be a
major power in Quebec society. This paralleled and was not unconnected with the declining birth rate. Both are characteristic of a
society that is growing wealthier and more educated. Put simply,
fewer people went to church, especially in the cities, and fewer
looked to the church for guidance in either religious or secular
matters. In no way is this more evident than in the questions of
abortion and birth control. Though the church is as opposed to
either as it ever was, increasing numbers of Quebeckers have
defied the dictates of their parish priests in both matters over the
last three decades. It is not unlike the pre-conquest days when the
people of New France honoured church dictates more in the
breach than in the observance.

The growth of the educated middle class also speeded up the
process of Americanization. Since the days of Papineau, the
United States has fascinated most Quebeckers. Where the
French scorn "English" Canada as a society that either doesn't
really exist or doesn't know it exists, they admire many things
about the United States, from its principles of political liberty to
its riot of consumerism. Put simply, American publications,
movies, and television programs have found a ready reception in
mainstream Quebec. Wealthy French Quebeckers send their
children to American schools and universities; not-so-wealthy
Quebeckers spend their vacations in Florida (where many communities have now posted French-language signs on their beach-
es). René Lévesque spent the Second World War as a war corre-
spondent with the U.S. Army and, soon after his election as premier in 1976, he spoke to the power brokers of Wall Street and
compared the drive of Quebeckers for independence to that of
the American colonists who threw the British out in 1776. This
must have surprised his audience, which probably thought of
him more as a Jefferson Davis leading the South out of the

union than as a George Washington. Thus American values have increasingly found a home in Quebec, a process that both accelerates and is accelerated by secularization. But in Quebec there is always a difference, and in this case it is a profound one: whereas the United States is a polyglot, pluralistic society, holding individual rights to be the only absolutes that the state has a duty to protect, Quebec is, by necessity and history, a society of cultural fundamentalism, holding that the collective rights of the French community are the prime absolute that the state has a duty to protect.

Quebec's tendency to be more secular, more American, more bourgeois, after 1945 established the ground for the Quiet Revolution. In turn, the Quiet Revolution pushed these tendencies even further. All the while Quebec's French communitarianism grew stronger. Where French society once stood on the three pillars of church, farm, and the French language, it now stands on one — language. Thus the community now defines itself only in cultural-linguistic terms. Two lines of defence are gone. Only one line of defence remains to preserve Quebec's distinctiveness in a North America (and a world) that is increasingly integrated. Nationalism is an inevitable by-product of a threatened community. Quebec not only feels threatened, it is threatened to some degree. With its birth rate in decline for much of the last three decades, with immigration to the rest of North America on the rise; with linguistic barriers failing all over the place; and with English emerging as the first truly global language of science, business, commerce, and transportation and communications, French Quebeckers are afraid that their distinctiveness may not survive much longer.

Is this a reason for Quebec to have more power within Canada? Here again our answer is no. First of all, Quebec already has all the constitutional power it needs to attack its falling birthrate. Second, if global factors originating outside Canada's borders threaten Quebec-within-Canada, they will threaten the State of Quebec even more. It will be *more* necessary for Quebeckers to speak English after secession than it is now, for example, because the global corporations with which Quebec will deal, and in which upwardly-mobile Quebeckers will want to work, do not have an Official Languages Act. We believe Quebec survival has always been best served within Canada and that anything which threatens the survival of Canada threatens Quebec. Nothing threatens Canadian survival more than a Quebec with special powers and special status.

As Quebec has changed since 1945, so has "English" Canada. Immigration has been one of the most important factors for change. Although the first major post-war wave of immigration was primarily white Europeans — war refugees from eastern and central Europe — later (and current) waves have brought hundreds of thousands of non-white immigrants from all over the globe. English-speaking Canada is, quite simply, no longer the white, British country it was purported to be as recently as 1945. Canada's new citizens have demanded not only an equal share of what Canada has to offer, but also to be treated as equals before the law. These demands ran counter to many of the conventions of Canadian life as they existed in 1945 and counter to some of the conventions that remain — the best example is that Catholics enjoy tax support for their schools in seven of ten provinces (a throwback to Confederation), but Sikhs, Hindus, Moslems, Jews, Buddhists, do not.

Like Quebeckers, English-speaking Canadians have also been affected by many of the values and conventions of American life. In no way is this more obvious than in the growth of the imperative to protect individual rights and, indeed, to elevate those rights over those of the group. The impulse produced its first concrete result with the adoption of the Canadian Bill of Rights in 1960 by the Diefenbaker government. Unlike the 1982 Charter of Rights and Freedoms, Diefenbaker's Bill of Rights was an ordinary statute of the federal government, and thus did not have any special status above other federal laws. But its passage by a government led by a man who did not believe in "hyphenated" Canadianism was a strong indication of the direction in which Canadian society was moving. That it came at the very time that the Quiet Revolution was also progressing so rapidly in Quebec ought to be instructive both to French Quebeckers and to Canadians.

The French of Quebec are often mystified by, even scornful of, the apparent lack of cultural shape of English-speaking Canada. Given their admiration of the United States, this is ironic, because no society lacks cultural shape as much as the United States. Culturally speaking, the United States is little more than thousands of diverse communities and hundreds of ethnic, racial, religious, and cultural groups linked by a common political system, by a common set of political values (for the most part), by economic self-interest, and by a mythology. All these attributes are, in fact, beginning to emerge in English-speaking Canada, and the Charter of Rights and Freedoms is playing a vital role in the process. English-speaking Canada's growing belief in liberal democracy is at the core of its newly emerging identity. But there will never be, and can never be, the sort of tight community of interest in English-speaking Canada that exists among the French of Quebec. That is also true in the United States. The fact is that democracies built upon immigration are very diverse places. This is their major weakness and their most significant strength. It allows for unfettered creativity in science, the arts, and culture on the one hand, while undermining the possibility of concerted political action on the other. It would have been far easier for "English" Canada to "give Quebec an answer" in 1940 than it is in 1990. But even in 1940 it would have been difficult because the veneer of a white, British Canada hid what was, even then, a very diverse country.

It is quite obvious now that English-speaking Canada did not know how to respond to the Quiet Revolution. It neither sympathized with nor understood what was happening, and no one knew the implications for the nation beyond Quebec. Thus its leaders did not know what to make of Quebec's sudden aggressiveness in the federal-provincial arena. As a result, serious mistakes were made. Nowhere was this more true than in the actions and inactions of the Liberal federal government led by Lester B. Pearson that was elected on April 8, 1963, and took office on April 22, two days after a sixty-five-year-old night watchman, Wilfred O'Neill, was killed by a terrorist bomb while making his rounds in an army recruiting centre in Montreal.

Pearson's first response to the Quiet Revolution was the Royal Commission on Bilingualism and Biculturalism, appointed in the third week of July 1963. The co-commissioners were André Laurendeau, a journalist who had been one of the leaders of the anticonscription movement in Quebec during the Second World War, and Davidson Dunton, president of Carleton University, from where much federal Liberal expertise has come. Four of the commissioners were francophone, four anglophone, and two were chosen from "other" groups in due recognition of the fact that not everybody in Canada could trace roots to France or Great Britain. Laurendeau had already documented and criticized the absence of French from the Canadian civil service. In a series of editorials in *Le Devoir*, Laurendeau had pointed out that unilingual English speakers found no language frontier, but that French speakers had to become fluently bilingual. One of the results, apparently, was that the French were alienated from Canada, or at least from the federal state. The one thing needful, therefore, was to increase the participation in the federal civil service by the French and to increase the use of the French language as well. In this way the myth of a Confederation bargain, the myth of dualism, could be reaffirmed under new circumstances. A second and subsidiary objective was to increase government support for the French language outside Quebec. The very premise upon which the commission was based determined the tone of its recommendations: Canada was a bicultural country. Since Canada was, and had been from the start (according to the B and B Commission), a bicultural society, its federal institutions had better start reflecting that fact or Canada's future as a united country was in doubt. That biculturalism, or its child, official bilingualism, had nothing to do with the Quiet Revolution; that Lesage, Lévesque, and the other leaders of Quebec were after more power *in Quebec* and would gladly have traded federal bilingualism for a greater piece of federal power (say, over immigration) did not faze Pearson in the least. Thus the B and B Commission proposed a basketful of solutions to problems of no serious *constitutional* import. And in doing so they laid the groundwork for official multiculturalism, for how could *anyone* be left out of the receiving line?

The second Pearsonian response was "co-operative" federalism — a federalism in which Ottawa approached all the provinces (it had to be all, lest Quebec be accorded a special status) more or less as equals in shaping the legislative future of Canada. As a diplomat and as a student of Canadian history, Pearson was inclined to seek the middle ground, to compromise, rather than to confront. He clearly believed that trying to pull in the reins was the worst way to keep Canada united. He probably thought there was some parallel to the British Empire in the late nineteenth century — the Empire had survived because the British had been flexible in responding to the demands for greater autonomy coming from the white colonies. Now it was time for Ottawa to be flexible with Quebec and, by definition, with the other provinces as well. But although Pearson's flexibility was clearly misguided — it aided Quebec's drive to special status and pushed Canada towards greater disunity, not less — it did not lead him to accept special status for Quebec. And when he brought the "three wise men" into his government in 1965 — Gérard Pelletier, Jean Marchand, and Pierre Trudeau — he brought three men who also rejected the idea of special status.

After two years of constant battles with Quebec, Pearson was much less inclined to be flexible. Following 1965 and the recruitment of the "three wise men," he attempted to change direction. These men, each of whom had impeccable credentials as a French nationalist and as a leading participant in the changes transforming Quebec, intended to revitalize the federal Liberal Party in Quebec and provide a new focus in Ottawa for the LaFontaine tradition. Pelletier was the editor of *La Presse*,

Quebec's most widely read newspaper; Marchand was the long-time leader of the Confédération des syndicats nationaux — the former Catholic union movement, which had become the most militant trade-union movement in Quebec; while Trudeau was a constitutional law expert, *bon vivant*, intellectual baiter of the Duplessis regime, and champion of liberal democracy in Quebec. With the entry of these men into the Pearson government — Marchand became minister of citizenship and immigration in December 1965, Pelletier became parliamentary secretary for the minister of external affairs in April 1967, and Trudeau became minister of justice in April 1967 — the federal Liberal Party stayed true to its LaFontaine traditions. It was prepared to transform Canada into a bicultural society, even to foist official bilingualism on the country, but it would not accord semi-statehood to Quebec. At least, not for the moment.

The Progressive Conservatives were another matter. As the perpetual official opposition party from the demise of the Borden-Meighen government in December 1921 until the Mulroney victory in September 1984, they developed a provincial-rights view of the world. That is typical in a federal system such as Canada's, where the governing party in Ottawa tends to view itself as the protector of federal prerogatives, and the opposition, whose job it is to oppose the government, sees things from the opposite perspective. It is no coincidence that most (though by no means all) of the great federal initiatives that have come in this century — the welfare state, the creation of a national airline, etc. — originated with the Liberals, who governed for most of the period from 1921 to 1984. Those that originated with the Conservatives, such as the Bank of Canada and the CBC, were expanded and enhanced by the Liberals.

The tendency of the Tories to side with the provinces in the ongoing federal-provincial tussle has been increased by their predilection for choosing former provincial premiers as party leaders. That was a natural consequence of their failure to produce successful federal politicians during their long interregnum. Whereas the federal Liberal Party has never had a former provincial premier as its leader, the Tories have had three of them since 1940 — John Bracken of Manitoba (1942-48), George Drew of Ontario (1948-56), and Robert Stanfield of Nova Scotia (1967-76).

The main reason why the federal Conservatives wandered in the political wilderness from 1921 until 1984 was their failure to make any permanent impact in Quebec. Borden's action on conscription killed the Conservative Party there. Although Quebec gave a majority of its seats to John Diefenbaker in 1958, this shift was temporary and represented Quebeckers' impulse to take out political insurance for themselves more than anything else. When the country swung back to the Liberals 1962-63, so too did Quebec voters. In short, the federal Liberals occupied the political centre in Quebec, and the federal Tories were forced to seek greener pastures elsewhere. Until 1960 they attempted to offset their unpopularity by championing the "Quebec First" policies of Duplessis. Even Diefenbaker, who had little understanding of — and less sympathy with — Quebec nationalism, tried to keep the Union Nationale-Tory axis alive.

The Tory abandonment of the John A. Macdonald vision of Canada began under the leadership of Robert Stanfield. On several occasions after his selection as party leader he espoused a special status for Quebec based on the notion that Canada was really *deux nations*. This was not surprising given that Diefenbaker and his "One Canada" vision had been done in by a coalition of Bay Streeters and Quebeckers with Stanfield as the beneficiary. But, as in many things, Stanfield waffled when his *deux nations* proclamations produced storms of protest in some quarters of the party. Stanfield was followed by Joe Clark, who tried to downplay the entire Quebec question during his time as leader of the Conservative Party, but who seemed to sketch (just barely) a decentralized vision of Canada as a "community of communities." He was never precise about the meaning of this vision, but it was clearly offered to the electorate in the 1979 federal election in opposition to Trudeau's supposedly highly centralized idea of Canada.

Clark's defeat in 1980 set the stage for Mulroney's accession to leadership of the party and, in 1984, to power. To succeed, Mulroney had to restore the Conservative Party to legitimacy in Quebec. The Tories already had a stranglehold on the West. If they could displace the Liberals in Quebec and take at least half of the rest of the country, they could achieve power. If they could sink deep roots in Quebec, they could keep it. Mulroney's strategy was to appeal to precisely those Quebeckers whom Trudeau had refused to do business with — the Papineau-style nationalists. Trudeau knew that they had wanted nothing from Canada but independence or something approximating it. That was why he thought no compromise with them was possible. Mulroney, on the other hand, saw them as the key to success. If the federal Tories could become the voice not of the LaFontaine nationalism that the Liberals already owned but of the Papineau nationalism that had been reinvigorated by the Quiet Revolution and the accession of the PQ to power in 1976, they could own Quebec. The Mulroney sweeps of Quebec in 1984 and 1988 were the result. Mulroney paid his debt to his nationalist allies with the Meech Lake Accord and acceptance by a federal government for the first time of the concept of special status for Quebec.

When Mulroney sent the life-giving electrical charge into the Meech Lake Frankenstein, the Liberals under John Turner and the New Democrats under Ed Broadbent should have opposed the manoeuvre with every ounce of strength in their bodies. Instead, they prostituted their principles for Quebec votes, embraced the Accord, and removed the possibility of choice from Canadian voters. Outflanked in Quebec by Mulroney's successful wooing of separatists such as Lucien Bouchard, Turner decided to try to outdo Mulroney at his own game. To a man who had felt overshadowed, betrayed, and embarrassed by his former leader, Pierre Elliott Trudeau, that must have been a relatively simple thing to do — teach Trudeau a lesson and try to dish Mulroney at the same time. But why did the New Democrats embrace Meech, when their social-democratic vision of Canada depended on a viable federal government? In some ways their support of the Meech Lake Accord and the special status it entailed was even more scandalous than that of the Turner Liberals, given their history and philosophical inclinations.

In fact, the NDP had flirted with the Papineau-style nationalists in Quebec since the mid-1960s. If the Tories had been wandering in the political wilderness in that province since the end of the First World War, the NDP and its predecessor, the CCF, had never even made the exodus from Egypt. From its founding in 1932 until 1990, no CCF or NDP candidate had ever won a seat, provincial or federal, in Quebec! The old CCF had built a small following among a handful of upper-middle-class English-speaking professors from McGill University and trade-union leaders in Montreal's working-class ridings, but the ardent opposition of the church and the strongly centralist nature of CCF policies had kept it far from the Quebec mainstream.

In the 1960s some Quebec New Democrats decided to attempt a breakthrough in that province by wooing left-wing separatists. The rationalization they used went something like this: "The separatists are really social democrats just like us except that they want to build social democracy only in Quebec." Thus left-wing Papineau-style nationalists found a warm and cosy spot inside the NDP and rapidly came to dominate the Quebec section of the party. It did not seem to matter that at the time they represented only themselves, because they were allotted the requisite slots to fill out the delegations that dutifully trooped off to the NDP's policy meetings every two years. Since New Democrats, by definition, are reasonable people who always choose the path of compromise, they began to shape their policies on national-unity issues to meet the requirements of the Quebec nationalists. When the left-wing Waffle Group grew within the party in the late 1960s, the tendency to pander to Quebec nationalism grew apace. At its 1967 policy convention, the party officially advocated "special status" for Quebec. As historian Desmond Morton observed: "it was the logical outcome of six years of resolutions."

In 1971 the NDP reversed its stand on Quebec at the same convention at which it selected old-time socialist David Lewis as party leader. The special-status platform plank had been a double-edged sword. Separatists had not been drawn to the party in sufficient numbers to make any difference during the 1968 federal election, but Trudeau's message of national unity had made special status into a millstone around the NDP's neck in English-speaking Canada. The NDP had learned nothing. Its soft spot for left-wing Quebec nationalism remained, and after the separatist Parti Québécois was founded in 1968, the hope burned in NDP hearts in Quebec that the party could make common cause with Lévesque and his followers. After Lévesque's victory in 1976, prominent NDP leaders such as John Harney, who had contested the 1971 leadership race, urged accommodation with Lévesque and did their best to sell sovereignty-association in English-speaking Canada. Harney and others thus laid the groundwork for the NDP's enthusiastic re-embrace of special status in the guise of the Meech Lake Accord. But whatever principles may have been involved in Broadbent's support for the accord, the prime consideration was the search for the elusive NDP seat in Quebec.

Canada has now been grappling with its constitutional mess for thirty years. At the beginning of the fateful decade of the 1960s, Diefenbaker's government made an attempt to patriate (transfer to Canada) the British North America Act, which had been a statute of the British Parliament. Although Canada gained full and formal independence in 1931 with the passing of the Statute of Westminster (also by the British Parliament), the BNA Act had never been patriated. That had not happened primarily because Ottawa and the provinces had been unable to agree on a formula for amending those parts of the act dealing with the federal-provincial division of powers. Diefenbaker's minister of justice, E. Davie Fulton, tried to devise a plan in 1960 but was not successful. He proposed a BNA Act that would have basically confirmed the status-quo division of powers and added an amending formula to it. Quebec, which had strongly supported Diefenbaker's initiative, rejected the Fulton plan because it did not give the provinces power over unemployment insurance, of all things. Diefenbaker wanted to bring the constitution home to Canada; Lesage wanted more power. Nothing was done for another three years.

In 1965 the Pearson Liberals revived constitutional discussions with the provinces over patriation. Building on the formula first proposed by Fulton, justice minister Guy Favreau and representatives of all ten provinces hammered out an agreement at Charlottetown in October 1964. Pearson was still in his "flexible" stage. The resulting "Fulton-Favreau" formula contained one major idea that had not been part of any previous constitutional proposals; if a group of provinces wished Ottawa to legislate in a field that was within provincial jurisdiction, such as medicare, they could delegate the power to do so to the federal government. If any province decided not to delegate those powers and to act on its own, it would receive financial compensation.

This formula had been devised by Claude Morin, Quebec's deputy minister of federal-provincial affairs. At that point Morin was a strong believer in special status (he later became a leading member of the Parti Québécois and a minister in both PQ governments), and he considered "opting out with compensation" to be the chief means of achieving that end. He would later believe that it would gradually lead to independence. The Quebec government adopted his position — Lesage was also a strong believer in special status — and won Favreau and the other provinces to its view using the argument that this would introduce a much-needed flexibility into the Canadian constitutional system. The Quebec leaders did not harp on their belief that opting out with compensation would lead to special status for Quebec. The deal was quickly done, and Pearson was able to announce that unanimous agreement had been reached on patriation with an amending formula. The Fulton-Favreau formula was supposed to be a typical Canadian compromise — all things to all people. It did not accord special status to Quebec, allowing Pearson and the other premiers to sell it in English-speaking Canada, but it did hold out the possibility of special status to Lesage, to Morin, and to those in Quebec who could appreciate the subtlety of it.

Quebec separatists didn't appreciate the subtlety. Since the formula clearly did not give Quebec the freedom to create the brand of autonomy they desired, they strongly attacked it. Opposition leader Daniel Johnson of the Union Nationale joined them, declaring that Quebec sought "equality" or independence. Journalists and intellectuals led the charge against ratification, and opposition quickly swelled even among the ranks of the Quebec Liberal Party. Although Lesage eventually convinced the party to support the formula, he soon got cold feet and failed to carry out his commitment to bring the measure before the Quebec legislature. Fulton-Favreau was dead by the fall of 1965. This was the first time that eleven governments had agreed on both patriation and key changes to the constitution. It was also the first of two times that a Quebec government had then changed its mind and rejected what it had previously accepted. Within two years Trudeau, with his strong opposition to special status, had replaced Favreau as minister of justice.

In his first term in office, Trudeau made one major effort to resolve the constitutional impasse. At a meeting of first ministers in Victoria in June 1971, he proposed patriation of the BNA Act, a limited bill of rights, official constitutional status for French and English, and a complicated amending formula designed to ensure that both Quebec and Ontario would always have a veto over constitutional change. The proposals went far towards integrating Quebec and the francophone community both inside and outside Quebec into Trudeau's brand of Henri Bourassa-style Canadian federalism. In this way, Trudeau hoped to end forever the demands for special status. Things turned out differently, though the initial compromise looked promising. For the very first time Quebec (and Ontario) were to have an absolute veto over constitutional change, thus elevating them above all other provinces. And French was to be given co-equal status with English. After three days of negotiations, all eleven governments agreed; when Quebec premier Robert Bourassa returned home, he met a storm of nationalist protest. Quebec had not got enough, his opponents declared. Bourassa reversed himself and started talking about "cultural sovereignty" and a "Canadian common market." Having killed the Victoria Charter, Bourassa then began to court the other premiers in the hopes of rallying their support for a common provincial control over all social policies, from family allowances to pensions. This was the second time that a Quebec government had given its assent to constitutional reform, only to reverse itself under pressure from extreme nationalists and then solicit support from power-hungry premiers. A pattern had been set. Clearly it was not enough for Quebec that the Victoria Charter created two provinces with special status.

Trudeau never lost his interest in constitutional issues, but nothing was, or could be, accomplished until the PQ government held its referendum in the spring of 1980. (Trudeau's only real accomplishment — if it can be called that — on the national-unity front between his election in 1968 and the 1980 referendum was the Official Languages Act of 1969, a child of the B and B Commission. The act declared the federal government officially bilingual and made the protection and preservation of bilingualism a priority for Ottawa.) After all, there was no point in discussing anything else if Quebec was going to go its own way. In seeking a mandate from Quebeckers to negotiate "sovereignty-association," Lévesque took the greatest gamble of his political life, and lost. When the voters denied him his mandate, the separatist option was, for a time, dead. That left the question of how he — a confirmed separatist — would play Trudeau's constitutional game.

The 1980 referendum led directly to the 1982 constitutional patriation and the Meech Lake Accord. All sorts of things have been written about the referendum and the promises made to Quebec by Trudeau during the campaign. It is claimed that Trudeau held out the hope of a special status for Quebec in trying to convince Quebeckers to vote *non*, but that is simply not true. The essence of that promise is supposed to have been made by Trudeau in a speech to a packed audience in Montreal's Paul Sauvé Arena on May 14, 1980, when he declared: "I can make a most solemn commitment that following a No vote, we will immediately take action to renew the constitution." But

Trudeau had already rejected the special-status vision of Canada espoused by Quebec Liberal Party leader Claude Ryan as, in fact, he had rejected special status all his life. To Trudeau, constitutional renewal meant a patriated, made-in-Canada constitution, with an entrenched charter of rights to protect individual liberties, and clauses entrenching Canada's bicultural, bilingual character. That was all he was prepared to concede to Quebec nationalism; that was all he thought Quebeckers could ever want or need. It is convenient but deceptive for the supporters of special status, including Prime Minister Mulroney, to claim that the Meech Lake Accord was an honest effort to repay a debt to Quebeckers that Trudeau had contracted that May evening in Montreal and had then left unpaid.

As soon as the results of the referendum were known, Trudeau moved to complete the patriation process. Initially he intended to go it alone if necessary, but the Supreme Court of Canada ruled that although it would have been legal in the strict sense for Ottawa to approach London on its own (in fact Ontario and New Brunswick supported Trudeau), it would have violated convention. Trudeau was forced to negotiate an agreement with the provinces; the Constitution Act, 1982, with its amending formula and Charter of Rights and Freedoms was the result. René Lévesque refused to agree to the deal struck at Ottawa in the fall of 1981, so Quebec's signature is not on Canada's current Constitution. The Meech Lake Accord was supposed to remedy that omission, even though the Constitution applies to all Canada, Quebec included, despite the absence of Lévesque's signature.

It was often stated during the Meech Lake debate that nothing could have induced Lévesque to sign the constitutional arrangement arrived at in Ottawa in the fall of 1981 because he was still a separatist, referendum or not, and was not interested in doing a deal with the rest of Canada. That is only half right. Up to the last night of negotiations, the proposals of the provinces had included a provision that a province would have the right to opt out of any future constitutional amendments giving Ottawa power to legislate in a field that had once belonged strictly to the provinces and receive compensation as if it were a full participant. The specific proposal came from Alberta; although the original idea had come from Claude Morin in 1964. When the final deal was cut in the wee small hours of November 4-5, 1981, Ottawa and nine provinces agreed to drop this idea of fiscal compensation. Lévesque, however, refused to do so and was left out in the cold. To him, fiscal compensation had always been the key to special status for Quebec:

> The right to opt out . . . is in my view a much superior weapon [to the veto], at one and the same time more flexible and more dynamic. "You wish to take this or that path we are not ready to follow? Very well, my friends, go ahead. But without us." From stage to stage. . . we could create something very like a country in that fashion.

In other words, Lévesque might well have signed a constitutional agreement in the fall of 1981, but only if it contained the one provision that he believed would eventually allow him to lead Quebec out of Canada. Since the final version of the Constitution Act would not open the road either to special status or independence for Quebec, it was not acceptable to Lévesque.

The Meech Lake Accord of 1987 would have ensconced special legal status for Quebec in the Canadian Constitution. It also revived the "opting out with compensation" that had been dropped in the fall of 1981. To entice Quebec to sign that constitution, Mulroney endorsed special legal status for Quebec. He was the first prime minister in Canadian history to do so. Since most of what Quebec demanded was also handed out to the other provinces at Meech Lake, they too agreed. Because John Turner got a chance to spit in Trudeau's face while trying to outdo the Quebec Tory nationalists, he too came on side. As a result of Ed Broadbent's desperate bid to make a breakthrough in Quebec, the NDP also joined the cabal. Thus, by the fall of 1987 the governing federal Tories, the opposition Liberals and New Democrats, and the premiers of all ten provinces had come to support special legal status for Quebec in the guise of Meech Lake. The genie was out of the bottle; Canada as we know it had started to come to an end.

4

FILING FOR DIVORCE

Time and again the premier of Quebec, the leader of the Parti Québécois, celebrity journalists on the CBC, and Prime Minister Mulroney himself declared: each provision of the Meech Lake Accord is sacrosanct, the distinct-society clause in particular, and the agreement constituted no more than the minimally acceptable terms to the Province of Quebec. Everybody knew this was coded Mulroney-speak for the French of Quebec. More precisely, it was the minimum that the Quebec nationalists said they would accept for the moment. But Canadians knew better. When the deal fell apart amid general rejoicing in the rest of the country, the precise reasons — from the established procedures of the Manitoba legislature to the personal style of Prime Minister Mulroney — no longer mattered very much. Perception was all. And Quebec nationalists perceived that they had been insulted, excluded, and rejected. They felt that they had made great concessions and that their flexibility and prudence had gone unrecognized. They had sacrificed their interests and their true desires for the good of Canada, and Canada had replied with a slap in the face. They had been willing to give federalism one last chance and they had been rebuffed. So they were indignant and angry. They still are.

For their part, Canadians were puzzled. It took some time for the implications to sink in. Quebec was angry and hurt; this Canadians knew. They were angry and hurt because their minimal demands proved too much for Canada to swallow; this Canadians knew as well. They were puzzled, however, because they had followed the logic of the Quebec nationalists' position and had come to the conclusion that it was easier to accept their maximum demands than their minimum ones. That is, independence, which everyone knew to be the maximum demand, was preferable to special legal status. This insight did not dawn all at once, and many politicians still have not figured it out, but that is the implication of the Quebec and the Canadian positions. The significance of the Meech Lake collapse, therefore, was that Canadians and Quebeckers had to face the real option of Quebec's departure from Canada. They did so and were not terrified by what they saw. Serious Quebec nationalists saw it as an opportunity to jettison the silly game of threatening to leave; Canadians saw it as an opportunity to jettison the interminable constitutional impasse. To put it another way, once it was clear that the minimal demands of Quebec for special status were unacceptable to Canadians, the terms of reference for the whole constitutional morass had changed forever. As we said at the end of the last chapter, the genie was out of the bottle and could never return.

The options are now clear in a way that they never have been before. The title of Daniel Johnson's 1965 book, *Egalité ou indépendance*, posed the alternatives as starkly as possible. The myth of dualism was based upon the assumption of equality between the French and everyone else — labelled, simply, "the English." But almost no one believes the myth any longer, for the very good reason that it corresponds not at all to the reality that the overwhelming majority of Canadians and Quebeckers experience on a daily basis. Old myths die hard, especially among those who seem to benefit by them. There will be voices

urging us to revert to the status quo ante Meech. They will coun-
sel Canadians to pretend that Meech Lake never happened.
They will tell us to ignore the genie. Many of our politicians no
doubt find this posture congenial. They, however, will soon be
overtaken by events. Very clearly, the thing cannot be undone.
The premise of equality between French and "English," or even
between Ottawa and Quebec City, is unacceptable to Canada,
whatever the opinions of the *bien pensants* of Quebec and
Ottawa.

The nationalist-federalist accommodation is dead. That leaves
only the option of independence. The government of Quebec
has evidently acknowledged this — not directly, but silently in
the terms of reference of the Bélanger-Campeau Commission.
The whole purpose of the exercise is to think through the implications of future and alternative relations between Canada and
Quebec. There would be no point if there was even a remote
chance of restoring the status quo. But there is none.

What, then, are we to make of the activities of the government
of Canada? It looks very much as if they are fiddling while Rome
burns. And as Leo Strauss once said of another group of dither-
ers, they are excused by two things: they don't know they are fiddling and they don't know Rome is burning. How else to explain
the advent of Keith Spicer's travelling sensitivity sessions?
Bélanger-Campeau proceeded on the basis of *de facto* sovereignty and bilateral relations between Quebec and Canada. In response
Prime Minister Mulroney invited Mr. Spicer to take to the road
and see what ailed the nation. The former head of the CRTC
and former language commissioner took off for Inuvik. After all,
he explained, that's where the country begins. Jack Webster, a
fellow commissioner, had the common sense to quit before his
reputation as an eccentric and crusty media personality was tar-
nished beyond repair.

Perhaps they are not fiddling. But then what is one to make of
the government's conversion to making bilateral deals with Quebec on such transparently national matters as immigration? Perhaps they still believe in dualism. Perhaps they are genuinely at a

loss over what to do. Perhaps they really do not know what the mood of the country is beyond the little world where, as Don Braid once said, the sun rises over the Château Laurier and sets beyond the Supreme Court Building. But we doubt it.

A more obvious explanation lies in the sheer existence of the Quebec caucus and in the career interests of the bureaucratic and political élite of this country. For all of them, the independence of Quebec would be personally disastrous. Apart from the nationalists in the Bloc Québécois, what is to become of the serried ranks of Quebec MPs? Where else in Canada would Brian Mulroney run? Where could he be elected? These are urgent and pressing matters if one happens to be an MP from Quebec. They are only slightly less so if one happens to be a Quebec deputy minister or ADM or similarly elevated Ottawa mandarin. Where will your career lead when the civil service of Canada no longer employs citizens from the state of Quebec? Can you really put your future in the hands of the Parti Québécois? Do you really want to be a Quebec civil servant? Even high-ranking English-speaking bureaucrats from Canada would have something to regret: all those wasted years learning French in order to qualify for a bilingual bonus!

In short, it is in the immediate interest of every Quebecker in Ottawa to keep Quebec in Canada. If they truly believe in the dualist myth, we can only apologize for shattering their dreams. Our remorse is lightened, however, by the observation that, whether they believe it or not, it is a myth that has served them well and served the rest of the country very badly indeed. Because the interests of a few, very powerful people in the nation's capital are at stake, the rest of the country should prepare itself for an enormous outpouring of blather and billingsgate. We can expect to be told, soon enough, that keeping these highly educated, well-qualified, certifiably bilingual civil servants employed is not only in the national interest, it is the national interest. In fact, we've heard it all before: without Quebec, Canada is lost; without Quebec, the entire country will go down or up the spout. We can expect to learn that what makes us great is official bilingualism and French on our cereal boxes. We will be sure to hear so much about the importance of national unity that even those simple souls who think it means something will be embarrassed by the sheer volume of codswallop. Alas, none of it will be true. Fortunately, little of it will be believed.

What, then, is to be done? Let us return to Daniel Johnson's alternatives: equality or independence. The meaning of the Meech Lake fiasco was that equality or something like it — special status for Quebec — was unacceptable to Canada. As we have argued already, it posed a fundamental threat to the foundations of liberal democracy in this country by creating two classes of citizens and two classes of governments. The pseudo option of pretending that nothing has changed is sheer self-deception, a dream world that dissolves under the slightest touch of reality. Which brings us again to independence. Here the image of divorce comes to mind.

We all know that marriages can fail. Some of us know that divorces can fail too. When they are bitter and protracted, they seem to benefit only the litigators and judges and maybe the psychiatrists and social workers who deal with the personal and social consequences. We have no desire to provide lawyers or members of the so-called helping professions with clients. We want a successful divorce, a quiet but final separation with no strings attached and all the loose ends tied up. There are no co-respondents and no one has cheated very much. Quebec has found continued participation in Canada intolerable and wishes to leave. "Irreconcilable differences" exist between the two parties, and so Quebec is suing for divorce. Canada should not contest it militarily or in the courts. The continued presence of Quebec in Canada does none of us credit and both countries harm.

What follows is a proposal. It is bound to be speculative. There is no expectation on our part that the process we outline here will be followed in every detail. But, in general, something like this will have to take place or we shall eventually be forced to confront much worse alternatives, including armed conflict. Canadians as well as Quebeckers must start thinking about the problems involved. And even if our thinking here is neither complete nor completely clear, it is a start. We are confident that our fellow citizens and our soon-to-be former fellow citizens will point out our errors soon enough.

Principles and Precedents

We might begin by raising the preliminary question of whether the imagery of marriage and divorce is altogether appropriate. First of all, who got married? Who is getting divorced? And how? Many Canadians are interested less in saving the marriage than in seeing that the estate is divided fairly. Who gets the house? Who gets the IBM stock? Who gets the cottage at Meech Lake?

Some of the representatives of the Parti Québécois seem to be of the view that English and French Canada are the parties to the divorce. But we have already seen more than once that the imagery of dualism and two founding races or peoples is fiction. This puts an intolerable strain on the notion that French and English Canadians could somehow agree to dissolve the Confederation pact or bargain, the as-it-were marriage contract. To be blunt: because there was no contract in the first place, there can be no successors to non-existent signatories.

We know that metaphorical divorce between parts of countries is very rare in recent history. There is a good reason for this. When two individuals wish to dissolve a legal marriage, there are legally unambiguous and straightforward procedures to be undertaken. Just ask any lawyer: a legal marriage can be legally dissolved because both marriage and divorce are governed by the law. There is no obvious legal analogue governing the association or disassociation of political bodies.

There are, however, a few principles and historical examples that might help clarify the issues. Let us begin with the principle of self-determination and the question of whether under international law the French of Quebec can legitimately have recourse to it.

The right of self-determination is the right of cohesive national groups — "peoples" — to choose for themselves a form of political organization and to determine their relation to other groups. Since a *cohesive* national group will inhabit a more or less well-defined territory, the right of self-determination also implies the right of a people living in a territory to determine the political and legal status of that territory. For example, a people may wish to establish their own state, to associate in federation, or to become part of another state. The principle first appeared after the First World War and was sporadically put into operation as part of the settlement process at the end of hostilities. The Treaty of Versailles in 1919, for example, provided for a plebiscite in Upper Silesia to determine whether it should be part of Poland or of Germany. Not until the end of the Second World War, however, and the inclusion of the principle in the U.N. Charter, has the right of self-determination and the associated right of self-government exercised much of an influence on international law.

Even if it is agreed that the principles of self-determination and self-government are inherently just and valid, it does not follow that they have any application to the French inhabitants of the Province of Quebec. Article 73 of the United Nations Charter provides a justification for the right of self-government, but it has been applied only to colonies of European powers or to "overseas provinces" of European states that were administered as colonies. Goa, for example, was administered as a colony though legally it was a province of Portugal; even so, Article 73 was held, quite properly, to apply. In contrast, Northern Ireland, with approximately the same legal status as Goa, has never been considered as suitable for the application of Article 73. And since the Province of Quebec has considerably more legal competence in Canada than does Northern Ireland in the United Kingdom, it is unlikely in the extreme that Article 73 could be applied to the French of the Province of Quebec. The same argument holds for the other anticolonial resolutions of the General Assembly.

More to the point, reliance upon U.N. declarations is a two-edged sword. The 1970 Declaration on Principles of International Law Concerning Friendly Relations (Declaration on Friendly Relations, for short), which has on occasion been invoked as having application to the French of the Province of Quebec, states among other things that "by virtue of the principle of equal rights and self-determination of peoples enshrined in the Charter of the United Nations, all people have the right freely to determine their political status." All member states of the U.N. are obliged to respect this right. The difficulty is as follows: if the French of the Province of Quebec are a "people" in the sense of the declaration, so too are the English of Quebec, to say nothing of the Cree, the Mohawks, and the Inuit. Only on the unwarranted assumption that Quebec is legally a French province would it make sense to invoke these U.N. principles. But legally Quebec is a province of Canada. Socially it is a pluralist society, not a French one. For this reason, the ancillary U.N. principles regarding the territorial integrity of ex-colonies that succeed in exercising the right of self-determination do not apply either.

This is an important consideration and we should be clear about its implications. First of all, an independent State of Quebec would not be an ex-colony of Canada. Its status as an ex-colony of France has no bearing on the problem. It has become accepted practice that when the inhabitants of a colony exercise their right to self-determination they constitute an independent state. By the same token, a colonial power retains sovereignty until it has allowed the colonial people to exercise that right. When they do and the colony becomes independent, it succeeds to the boundaries of the former colonial power even though it may not find them agreeable. The usual reason why post-colonial boundaries are not entirely satisfactory is because pre-independence colonial boundaries often conflict with the principle of self-determination by artificially dividing an ethnic and cultural group. French inhabitants of Canada outside the Province of Quebec would provide an appropriate analogy. The principle involved in the decolonization experience, however, is rather different; namely, in practice as well as according to international law, the principle of automatic sovereign succession overrides the principle of self-determination.

We do not believe, therefore, that the precedents of the decolonization experience apply to the secession of the State of Quebec. Nor, *a fortiori*, do U.N. General Assembly resolutions regarding wars of national liberation apply. These were opposed by Western states, including Canada, and were passed as a result of majorities assembled from communist and Afro-Asian states. They have no bearing at all on the question of the legal and peaceful separation of Quebec and Canada.

It is for these and other similar reasons that Professor Jacques Brossard, the foremost *péquiste* constitutional expert, dismissed the several U.N. resolutions dealing with self-determination in the context of decolonization as being inapplicable to Quebec. We agree. Under international law, therefore, we maintain that there is no instrument to guide the transition of the Province of Quebec to independence. In principle there is no validity whatsoever to the claim of the French to an independent state. None of the post-war U.N. resolutions against colonialism is relevant. In particular, the 1970 Declaration on Friendly Relations acknowledges no obligation of existing states to endow ethnic minorities with their own state by means of partitioning the existing state. It does, on the contrary, reaffirm the territorial integrity and political unity of existing states. French aspirations might receive partial acknowledgement under international law if their human rights were systematically violated, but that acknowledgement would have only political force. It would have no legal force. So long as Canada does not systematically discriminate on the basis of race, creed, or colour, international law recognizes no demands for legitimate secession. And, in fact, if discrimination exists in the practice of the Government of Canada it amounts to *de facto* discrimination in favour of the French, as a result of implementing the policy of official bilingualism. In any event, the plain meaning of the U.N. resolutions would explicitly assign all problems of ethnic self-determination to the internal political and constitutional processes of Canada.

Other historical precedents regarding the creation of states through peaceful secession are also not very helpful, though certain superficial similarities do exist. In 1905, for example, Norway gained its independence from Sweden; in 1960, Senegal and Mali split; in 1965 Singapore left the Malaysian federation. Closer attention to the details and conditions of these examples, however, indicates that they have very little bearing on our current difficulties. The union of Norway and Sweden joined two equal kingdoms under a single sovereign. Mali was a federation of sovereign states and therefore included the right to secede at will. The Singapore example is more promising insofar as the culturally and ethnically distinct island was invited by the federal Malaysian government to leave. However, unlike Quebec, Singapore was considerably more prosperous than the rest of the federation. Moreover, it had belonged to the federation for the comparatively short period of two years. In addition, there are the provisions under Article 17 of the Soviet constitution, which allows any constituent republic to secede from the U.S.S.R. None has done so at the time of writing.

The conclusion we would draw from this evidence from the wider world is that we are on our own. The political reason is not a great mystery. Usually states that are recognized as independent by other states in the world are reluctant to allow part of their population and territory to secede. The argument against secession is that it would inevitably mean a diminution in the unified state's wealth, resources, and power. By being so diminished the successor state would command a lower international profile and exercise less influence on international affairs, enjoy a lower standard of living, and so on. On occasion, states oppose secessionist movements because they entail the creation of a hostile neighbour on its new and constricted borders.

None of these arguments has any relevance to the secession of Quebec from Canada. By ending the wasteful transaction costs of official bilingualism and especially the ongoing transfer of wealth from Canada to Quebec, the citizens of Canada would undoubtedly be more wealthy, not less. The citizens of Quebec under the new regime would, we hope, prosper as well. So far as we can see, the only losers would be the handful of civil servants who administer these misbegotten policies. Canada, it is true, would lose some of its current resource base and population. But resources are largely under provincial jurisdiction anyway. The loss of the population of Quebec would be unlikely to entail any loss of markets and, more important, it would mean no loss of power. On the contrary, both Canada and Quebec would emerge internally more united. The secession of Quebec would bring to an end the debilitating and hopeless series of conferences that attempt to square the constitutional circle. Power is not a fixed commodity, so that if one country grows more powerful another one must grow weaker. Both Canada and Quebec would emerge more powerful because both would have abandoned the one aspect of their cohabitation that weakens them both — the impossibility of finding a legal formula to express a real social and political contradiction. The law may be many things, and it can abide a good deal of ambiguity. It cannot, however, contradict itself, as it does today: Quebec cannot be part of a country dedicated to the principles of liberal democracy and at the same time be faithful to its nationalist vision. As an independent country, however, the tensions between Quebec nationalism and liberal democracy will diminish, even if they do not entirely disappear. To recall what we said earlier: we have every expectation and every hope that an independent Quebec would be a liberal democracy. We believe that the damage being done to liberal democracy in both Canada and Quebec is in large measure a consequence of the unworkable constitutional regime under which we all suffer at present. Apart we have the opportunity to flourish; together we can only grow increasingly discontented.

As we have said, international law, international practice, and U.N. anticolonial resolutions are of virtually no assistance in defining the procedures of separation. If we look to Canadian constitutional law there is, not surprisingly, no provision for provincial secession. On the contrary, most of the relevant sections of the Constitution contemplate the addition, not the subtraction, of provinces. The BNA Act of 1871, for example, gives power to the Parliament of Canada to establish new provinces "in any territories forming for the time being part of the Dominion of Canada, but not included in any Province thereof" (sec. 2). Parliament also has the power to "increase, diminish, or otherwise alter" the borders of any province, but only "upon such terms and conditions as may be agreed to" by the legislature of that province. The purpose of these provisions, as was made explicit in the preamble, was to dispel any doubts about the capacity of Parliament to create or establish new provinces in Rupert's Land and the North-Western Territory. The actual territory involved extended from the watershed of Hudson Bay to the Arctic Ocean, and westward from the Great Lakes watershed to British Columbia. On the basis of this act, large *tranches* of Rupert's Land were added to Quebec in 1898 and again in 1912. Nothing was said either in the act of 1871 or in the legislation expanding the borders of Quebec about the consequences of secession.

Another tack may be to consider the secession of Quebec as a simple change in provincial boundaries for which provision has been made in the Constitution. In sections 42 and 43 of the Constitution Act, 1982, we may find some more promising legal formulae. But even here the apparent meaning of these sections would have to be stretched. Section 42(1) lists six matters that can be amended in accordance with the general amending procedure of Section 38(1). That procedure requires the agreement of two-thirds of the provinces with 50 per cent of the population for a constitutional amendment to occur. This is usually identified as the seven-fifty formula (seven provinces, 50 per cent). Subsection (f) states: "notwithstanding any other law or practice, the establishment of new provinces" can be undertaken according to the seven-fifty provisions. Now, since Subsection (e) governs the extension of existing territories into provinces, Subsection (f) must contemplate either the establishment of new provinces from existing provinces uniting together, as has been suggested from time to time regarding Atlantic Canada, or the establishment of new provinces by dividing existing provinces.

So far as the unification of existing provinces into a larger province is concerned, this procedure would also be subject to the provisions of Section 43(a), which indicates that "any alteration to the boundaries between provinces" would be subject to authorization by Parliament and by "the legislative assembly of each province to which the amendment applies." If there was proposed an alteration not to the boundary between provinces but between one province and the United States, this amendment would, one assumes, be subject to the seven-fifty provisions of the general amending procedure of Section 38(1). There would, in this case, be no alteration to the boundaries between provinces but only to the boundary of a single province. By the same logic, it ought to be possible to establish a new province within the boundaries of an existing province if it can be done in such a way as to avoid any alterations in the boundary of any other province. If this interpretation is accurate, it might be possible to create a province out of the Lower Mainland of British Columbia, out of Metro Toronto, or, indeed, out of the Lower North Shore of Quebec, by using the general amending procedure. The same procedure would be used to determine the number of senators and, perhaps, of MPs. Moreover, it would be possible to do so *without the consent* of the province involved, provided the conditions specified in Section 38(1) were met.

Unfortunately, this legal end-run could not be executed in the specific instance of finding a legal means to achieve the independence of Quebec according to established constitutional procedures. Any alteration of the provincial boundaries except for part of the South Shore and the Eastern Townships would require the consent of the neighbouring provinces, Newfoundland, New Brunswick, and Ontario. There is no provision in the Constitution for dealing with the possibility of changing a provincial boundary shared with another province when one of the provinces involved objects. We have every reason to believe that, for one reason or another, the provincial governments (including the Government of the Province of Quebec) would so object. In a word, the Constitution does not provide for the possibility of secession.

It is necessary, therefore, to resort to extra-constitutional procedures. This is a very serious step to take because it amounts to something like a revolutionary founding or refounding of the regime. Not only has such an act never been taken in Canadian history, but much of our history has been devoted to the rejection of such acts. Canadians have gone to great lengths to stress the continuity of their constitution with the ancient law of Great Britain. Some Canadians have gone so far as to consider this legal tradition an important ground upon which to distinguish their political culture from that of the United States. But in the absence of international and national legal procedures it would seem we have no choice but to invent our own.

The Procedure

In the absence of generally agreed-upon legal or constitutional guidelines, we propose a three-phase procedure by which Canada would accept the independence of Quebec. The first step is for the National Assembly of the Province of Quebec to declare itself to be the *de facto* Government of the State of Quebec. The second step is for the Government of Canada immediately to grant *de facto* recognition to the State of Quebec. The third step is to commence negotiations to resolve any outstanding differences, following which Canada would extend *de jure* recognition to Quebec and establish full diplomatic relations. An alternative to the somewhat obsolescent *de facto/de jure* distinction would be, in phase two, to establish "dealings" or *relations officieuses* with the authorities in Quebec prior to establishing diplomatic relations.

In relation to this procedure one matter at least is very clear: Quebec cannot negotiate independence and sovereignty, it can only declare it. The attempt to negotiate sovereignty is, very clearly, indistinguishable from a bluff. A declaration at the very least indicates to the government and citizens of Canada that Quebec is very serious about independence and is not at all interested in the pursuit of loose federalism by other means. Loose federalism is what got us all into this mess; even looser federalism would turn a bog into quicksand. As we stated earlier, separation, sovereignty, and independence can only be goals, not bargaining ploys or threats. A declaration of independence is the only procedure worthy of the national dignity of the French of North America. Let us, then, consider the issues. Questions of renewed federalism can no longer possibly be relevant.

The criteria for statehood that are generally recognized in customary international law were conveniently set forth in the Montevideo Convention of 1933 on the Rights and Duties of States. Article 1 declared that a state possessed four attributes: a permanent population, a defined territory, a government, and a capacity to enter into relations with other states. There is no difficulty as regards the criterion of a permanent population: Quebec is not a nomadic society. Second, a defined territory does not initially require fixed frontiers. As the United States argued in 1948 in support of the admission of Israel to the United Nations, many states began their existence with unsettled frontiers. This was true of the United States itself and, for analogous reasons, it would be true of the State of Quebec as well. In other words, one of the "outstanding differences" to be settled prior to the establishment of diplomatic relations would be the international frontier between the two countries.

The State of Quebec would, we assume, have a government. We expect it would be constituted in and by the National Assembly of the former Province of Quebec. That government would be sovereign and so would be capable of establishing relations with other states. The last two criteria of the Montivideo Convention are closely connected but not identical. The third, the attribute of government, is largely a matter of internal sovereignty; the fourth is concerned more with external legal relations between the new entity and existing states and involves the *de facto/de jure* distinction mentioned earlier.

The case of Southern Rhodesia illustrates the distinction between the third and fourth criteria. As a self-governing British colony prior to 1965, Southern Rhodesia met the first three criteria for statehood: population, territory, and government. By declaring unilateral independence, it clearly was attempting to meet the fourth criterion as well. As a consequence of a U.N. Security Council directive, all U.N. member states except South Africa refused diplomatic relations with it. Most international legal experts agreed that Southern Rhodesia was not a state, though their reasons for agreement tended to vary. So far as Quebec is concerned, it would be necessary for Canada to recognize both the government and the state. Recognition of the former would acknowledge the extra-constitutional event that produced the new regime in the former Canadian province; recognition of the latter would acknowledge the international legal personality of Quebec and so enable the resolution of outstanding differences and full diplomatic recognition to proceed.

Recognition of governments typically involves difficulties and ambiguities when a new regime takes power unconstitutionally, by violence or with foreign help. Necessarily the State of Quebec will be founded unconstitutionally, but that fact should not lead to grave difficulties. The difficulties lie in the area of conflicting interests, establishing frontiers, principles of economic association, and so on. And these are sufficiently grave that it would not be in Canada's interest to accord full diplomatic recognition immediately. This is a common practice in international affairs when one country wishes to avoid endorsing all the claims of another, and yet cannot avoid acknowledging its existence. There are, then, two aspects to recognition: the first is, so to speak, objective, in that the new regime is acknowledged as exercising the powers of government. The second depends on the behaviour of the new regime and hinges on such matters as provision of internal democracy, obedience to international law, fulfilment of treaty obligations, payment of international debts, respect for human rights, and so on.

The first aspect has traditionally been identified with *de facto* recognition. It is generally accorded to a government that exercises control over at least part of a state's territory but that does not enjoy uncontested authority. A *de jure* government would have the full legitimacy that comes from being the rightful government of a state. This is why we propose that Canada immediately extend the former recognition to Quebec and grant *de jure* recognition following the successful negotiation of the terms of independence.

Negotiating Independence

Conferring *de jure* recognition is a formality. We subscribe to the view of Winston Churchill, that "the reason for having diplomatic relations is not to confer a compliment but to secure a convenience." *De jure* recognition would simply acknowledge that the initial outstanding difficulties attendant upon the division of Canada had been settled.

Before considering those difficulties and elaborating what we believe ought to be the Canadian position, we must first indicate who are the parties to the negotiations. On the Quebec side we assume that the same government that issued its declaration of independence will accredit the appropriate negotiators. Unless the current cohort of Quebec MPs plans to act like the octogenarian members of the Kuomingtang on Taiwan, dreaming they represent Shanghai and Beijing, they would immediately be eligible to receive their generous parliamentary pensions. It is likely that a new Government of Canada would have to be formed once the seventy-five MPs from Quebec no longer represented constituencies in Canada. This government would appoint its negotiators. No doubt it would be prudent not to call an immediate election; it would also be wise to consult extensively but unofficially with the provincial governments and with other interested parties.

Section 108 of the BNA Act, 1867, dealt with the transfer of property from the pre-Confederation provinces to the Dominion. The property involved was enumerated as Schedule III to the act and concerned canals, harbours, lighthouses, railways, public buildings, and so on. A similar enumeration of public property could be drawn up with comparative ease. The difference between then and now is that now Quebec is seceding from Canada, not joining it. Accordingly, Quebec has no claim on any federal property outside Quebec. Canada, has, however, clear title to and claim on all improvements made to federal property inside Quebec since Confederation. Likewise, the relative allocation of responsibility for the public debt, the co-ordination of fiscal divestments, and other matters of a more or less technical nature can probably be safely left to civil servants, but only because Quebec will need to meet its financial obligations to Canada if it is to retain any credibility in international financial circles. In other words, we do not put our trust in Jacques Parizeau as a nice guy, but in Jacques Parizeau as a canny economist.

In the definition of the international boundary between Quebec and Canada, however, political principles as well as national interests are involved. In particular, there exists a widespread misapprehension in the Province of Quebec that the State of Quebec will have more or less the same borders as the Canadian province. Canada has no reason to accept this assumption as valid; there are excellent historical, legal, and political reasons to dismiss it out of hand. Such a claim may be intelligible in terms of the national interest of Quebec, but that is of no concern to Canada. Indeed, Canadian national interests are, in this regard, unalterably opposed to those of the State of Quebec. The only grounds of principle upon which such a claim could be based is that Quebec is a colony of Canada, and so, like Nigeria or Kenya, should inherit colonial frontiers. But we have already shown that this argument is irrelevant. Quebec is not and never has been a colony of Canada. If, therefore, colonial precedents are to be invoked, the boundaries of New France in 1763, not the current provincial boundaries, would be the place to start. Those borders defined a colony along the left bank of the St. Lawrence River, and the north shore of Lake Ontario. In other words, the *only* boundary to which Quebec has even the shadow of a historical claim is the boundary of New France.

A second misapprehension concerns the question of how Quebec came to exercise jurisdiction over the northern two-thirds of the province. Labrador and Rupert's Land were never French and so were never ceded by France to Britain. If this point is sometimes overlooked, the reason, no doubt, is that no one has ever taken seriously the prospect of negotiating Canada's frontier with Quebec. Rupert's Land was defined in British law as consisting of the territory included in the Hudson Bay drainage basin. Labrador extended from the eastern height of Rupert's Land to the Atlantic Ocean. Very simply, these lands were British long before the 1763 Treaty of Paris confirmed them. In the late seventeenth century, it is true, the Hudson's Bay Company engaged in a prolonged dispute with France over forts along the coast and had to struggle against interlopers from the south, but these were informal and irregular conflicts among fur traders. All Rupert's Land remained British except for a period of seventeen years, between 1697 and 1713, during which time several Hudson's Bay Company forts were occupied by French traders. After the Treaty of Utrecht in 1713, France made no serious claims to any part of Rupert's Land.

Quebec, however, has made serious claims on Canadian territory. To begin with, Quebec has never accepted the decision of the Judicial Committee of the Privy Council of 1927 that established its boundary with Labrador. In fact, Quebec has as much a claim to Labrador as it does to upstate New York, and a much better claim to southern Ontario, which was genuinely a French possession prior to 1763. So far as Canada is concerned, there is nothing to discuss regarding Labrador.

Nor does the claim by an independent Quebec to the territory that constituted Rupert's Land have any validity. Between

1841 and 1867, as has been pointed out, territory now included in the southern parts of the provinces of Ontario and Quebec formed the single colony of Canada. The border between Canada and Rupert's Land at that time was real, and it was enforced. By no means was it a mere line on a map. One of the chief sources of revenue for any nineteenth-century British colony was an excise tax levied on imported goods; a second was customs duty. During the nineteenth century, as in the twentieth, the Hudson's Bay Company had no interest in paying any more taxes than it was forced to by government authorities. For years the company used its incomparable knowledge of the north to bring goods through Hudson Bay into the colony of Canada. By mid-century, however, Canada had determined that revenue lost to smuggling was greater than the expense of defending its northern frontier, and so erected a string of customs-inspection stations to collect excise tax and duties on goods imported from Rupert's Land.

Not only was Rupert's Land a territory politically distinct from the colony of Canada, but the manner of its acquisition by Canada underlined its distinctiveness. In 1868, a year after Confederation, the British Parliament passed the Rupert's Land Act, specifying that the Hudson's Bay Company would surrender its "lands rights, privileges, liberties, franchises, powers and authorities" under certain terms and conditions to be negotiated by the company, the Colonial Office, and the Canadian government. The negotiations were protracted, and the specification of the terms and conditions took years of haggling between company shareholders and the company, between the company and the Colonial Office, between the Colonial Office and Canada, and between Canada and the company. Some of these disputes erupted into lawsuits. In the background there remained the unacknowledged claims of the inhabitants of the Red River Settlement who were decidedly cool about being incorporated into Canada. Neither they nor the other natives of Rupert's Land were consulted about their new status.

Rupert's Land was not, therefore, on the market the way Alaska had been a few years earlier. A good number of Hudson's Bay Company stockholders wished to sell Rupert's Land to the highest bidder and hoped to begin the auction with an offer from China. Russia and the U.S.A. were also expected to get in on the action, along with Canada. Some Canadian politicians spoke of the purchase of Rupert's Land. Some Canadian historians still do. But in fact the transfer of Rupert's Land to Canada was not a real-estate deal. The Crown in right of Great Britain simply transferred its territory to the Crown in right of Canada. Canada "indemnified," which is a polite way of saying bought off, the Hudson's Bay Company not for the *territory* of Rupert's Land but for the several capital improvements made on it during the course of "the Company's sway" over the previous 230 years.

Looked at from the perspective of Canadian national history, Rupert's Land was a gift to the new Confederation by the Crown. It was, so to speak, the missing link between Canada and the British Pacific colony of British Columbia. Once Rupert's Land was added to Canada it made sense to the empire builders of the Macdonald-Cartier coalition to extend the new eastern confederation to the Pacific, to build the CPR, and to include British Columbia. So far as Rupert's Land to the east of Hudson Bay was concerned, the North-East Territories as they were called in the 1880s, very little was expected of them by way of commercial viability. It was fur territory peopled by aboriginal natives and barbaric fur traders, as it had been for centuries.

During the 1880s, in both Quebec and Ontario, civil servants, anxious as ever to increase their control over humans and the territory on which they live, agitated for the extension northward of their provincial borders. As was noted earlier, in 1898 the first slice of Rupert's Land was added to the two provinces carved from the old colony of Canada. Again in 1912, Quebec and Ontario civil servants were the force behind the further extension northward of the Quebec border.

The conclusion we would draw from these historical facts is as obvious as it is simple: Quebec gained legal title to the territory formerly comprising a portion of Rupert's Land *only* and *solely* because it was a Canadian province. There is no other conceivable basis for Quebec to advance its claim. Its administrative jurisdiction, therefore, is contingent upon its remaining a province of Canada. In other words, Quebec gained jurisdiction over these lands by virtue of its being part of Canada and on the assumption that the lands would remain Canadian territory. The northward expansion of the frontiers of Ontario and Quebec, therefore, was simply a matter of transferring jurisdiction over Canadian territory from the Crown in right of Canada to the Crown in right of a Canadian province. When Quebec leaves Canada it surrenders all territory it gained while it was part of Canada.

In any event, the Province of Quebec has historically been reluctant to exercise its administrative responsibilities in the area. Indeed, prior to 1960 the government of Quebec was virtually non-existent so far as the inhabitants of the territory formerly included in Rupert's Land were concerned. As late as 1939, the government of Quebec argued in the Supreme Court of Canada that native people were the responsibility of the Dominion government. The case involved compensation to the Hudson's Bay Company for having fed the native people, during 1938, in order to keep them from starving. The company presented its bill to Quebec and was unceremoniously told to go to Ottawa. The Supreme Court decided in Quebec's favour: Ottawa had responsibility. Ottawa would pay.

Historically, therefore, Rupert's Land is Canadian territory. The separation of Quebec and Canada cannot be undertaken on the basis of the territorial integrity of the Province of Quebec. Certainly the Government of Canada has no right to cede Canadian territory to a foreign power. Concerning the assets currently in place in the former territory of Rupert's Land that owe their existence to action undertaken by the government of the Province of Quebec or by Quebec investors, the precedents established in the negotiations between the Hudson's Bay Company, the Colonial Office, and Canada would apply. Canada and Quebec would, therefore, negotiate an "indemnification" package to compensate Quebec for such major capital projects as the James Bay hydro-electric developments and the iron-ore railway to Schefferville. With James Bay in particular, it seems both reasonable and to the benefit of Canada and Quebec to negotiate transmission corridors from Canada through the State of Quebec to markets in Ontario and the U.S.A. Alternatively, Canada might sell the power to Hydro-Québec, as Newfoundland has done with power from Churchill Falls, Labrador. The terms and conditions, however, would be more equitable than those of the Churchill Falls deal. But these are details to be worked out during the horse-trading phase of the separation process. No doubt Ontario Hydro could supply any expert staff needed to keep the electricity from James Bay flowing, and the RCMP would provide security for the resident population. We are chiefly concerned, however, with principles, not details, and in principle, ownership of these capital improvements to Rupert's Land, like *ownership* of the capital improvements undertaken by the Hudson's Bay Company during the nineteenth century, is simply not an issue to be discussed. Indemnification is negotiable now as it was then.

During the 1950s, when Marcel Chaput first explained "why he was a separatist," the arguments and aspirations of men and women in favour of an independent state ignored the possibility that the new state would pose a threat to the interests of Canada or to the interests of the United States. In the short term, no doubt, the State of Quebec would threaten no one. Canadian and American policy makers could take some comfort in the words of spokesmen for a hypothetically independent state that expressed their expectations of friendly relations among the three North American states. But foreign policy, and especially strategic-defence policy, is formulated not on the basis of stated intentions but on the basis of perceived capacities. Not declarations of undying friendship but perceptions of the possibility of a threat to one's national interest are the foundation of sound policy. "Covenants without the sword," said the greatest English political philosopher, Thomas Hobbes, "are but words." An independent Quebec, at least one that possessed the same borders as the Province of Quebec, would certainly pose problems for Canadian and American strategic defence. This fact was pointed out to Chaput and the early separatist dreamers in a classic statement by André Laurendeau in 1955. Splitting Canada into three pieces, he said, would reduce Atlantic Canada to "a small isolated territory, incapable of supporting itself. Western and Central Canada would lack an outlet to the Atlantic. The whole of the Canadian people would never freely consent to such a breakup." And indeed, as Laurendeau said, such a state would prove intolerable to Canada's vital national interests.

The reason why the existence of a foreign state athwart the St. Lawrence would be unacceptable to Canada is obvious from a glance at a map. Territorial contiguity is, very simply, a vital Canadian national interest. Professor Jacques Brossard has addressed the matter of territory and has come up with an imaginative solution. According to him, there would really be no break in Canadian territory since Ontario could communicate directly with Nova Scotia by way of Hudson Strait. Even if one were to overlook the disputed question of whether Hudson Strait is Canadian or international waters, to propose that a water route from Churchill or Moose Factory to Atlantic Canada is "direct" is preposterous and unacceptable.

The fact is, the separatists contemplate a break between the current Ontario-Quebec border and the New Brunswick-Quebec border. The territory of Atlantic Canada would become, for all practical purposes, an exclave of Canada. The experience of European nations regarding enclaves (or exclaves) of territory requiring passage through a foreign state indicates that a general, though not a universal, right of passage exists. Private and civilian government officials are normally allowed free access from the home state to the enclave to perform normal private and official tasks. Free access is usually denied when the home state seeks to send military forces into the enclave. It is clear that a sovereign Quebec capable of interdicting the movement of military equipment to Canadian Forces bases in Atlantic Canada would be unacceptable to Canada.

The arguments made by spokesmen for Quebec all assume that, as with Rupert's Land, the State of Quebec would inherit the territory south of the St. Lawrence River. But this is a false assumption as well. Not only would it not be in Canada's national interest to allow any territorial break, but in fact Quebec has no claim to the South Shore independent of its status as a British possession or Canadian province.

The South Shore was first defined as part of Quebec in 1763. By the Treaty of Paris, the colony of Canada was extended to include parts or all of the "antient colonies of Nova Scotia, New England and New York." That is, Quebec was extended south of the St. Lawrence River into territory that had traditionally been English. The State of Quebec has therefore as much a right to the Eastern Townships and the South Shore as it has to upstate New York, namely none. By the Treaty of Utrecht, 1713, for instance, France acknowledged British sovereignty over all the lands of the Iroquois Confederacy. The Khanawake Reserve at the south end of the Mercier Bridge, made famous during the summer of 1990, is a sharp reminder that Iroquois lands extended to the south shore. By European lights, this meant they were British, not French. The Mohawks, we now know, have their own views on this question. It is true that the extent of Iroquois lands was in dispute. It is also true that, during the 1750s, following the Treaty of Aix-la-Chapelle, French and British negotiations over a frontier proved inconclusive. Later negotiations took place in light of the outcome of the Seven Years War, which resulted in the Treaty of Paris. In short, while the southern boundary of the Province of Quebec with the U.S.A and New Brunswick is entirely legitimate, it has no value whatsoever as a southern boundary of the State of Quebec. As with Rupert's Land, those territories were added, for reasons of administrative convenience, to one British territory from another. Since the Crown in Right of Canada is the legitimate successor to British imperial possessions, territories added to the British colony of Quebec need not be ceded to a foreign government by Canada, especially when they are of such strategic importance to Canada.

The Seaway and communication with Atlantic Canada make Canadian possession of the south shore of the St. Lawrence imperative.

Other territorial adjustments of less national interest to Canada but of great immediate interest to Canadians currently living in Quebec would include the Ottawa Valley and the Lower North Shore of the St. Lawrence, which is peopled mostly by Newfoundlanders and Channel Islanders. The same can be said of parts of the west end of Montreal Island. The political principle to be invoked here is that if the French claim, on ethnic and cultural grounds, a right to secede from Canada, then the non-French have such a right to secede from Quebec. What is sauce for the goose is sauce for the gander.

In 1980 William F. Shaw and Lionel Albert argued in their book *Partition: The Price of Quebec's Independence* that the separation of Quebec and Canada would never occur because the French people of that province would not pay the price. This argument was echoed by many politicians during the referendum campaign that same year. The premiers of Alberta and Saskatchewan emphasized that Quebec would be treated as a foreign country, so separation was unthinkable. The premier of Ontario said that his province would never negotiate any form of association with Quebec, so separation was unthinkable. Jean Chrétien orchestrated a multimillion dollar public-relations campaign indicating how much Quebec benefited from Confederation, so separation was unthinkable. We agree with all these statements of fact, but draw the opposite conclusion. We believe separation is necessary even though the cost might be substantial. Only the intellectuals at the head of the Parti Québécois could look with equanimity on the cost of separation. And they, precisely, will be the ones who will not have to shoulder the costs because they will be the new bureaucratic élite, in control — they fervently expect — of a flourishing new country. Neither we nor anyone else can know whether an independent Quebec will flourish. We are not as sanguine as the leaders of the PQ but, for the sake of the French in Quebec, we hope that a sovereign Quebec will be at least as prosperous as the province.

However this may be, of one thing there can be no doubt. As a result of Quebec's own actions, the political as well as the economic cost to Canada of keeping Quebec within its borders is now unnecessarily and unacceptably high. When the alternatives in the real world are equality or independence, the choice is clear. With independence will come just the equality that sovereign states possess: formal, legal equality. Gone forever will be the pretence of the Quebec nationalists that Quebec could ever enjoy substantive equality or anything approaching it within Canada. Nothing like the dual-monarchy along the lines of the Hapsburg Empire is even remotely connected to the Canadian reality. The separation of Quebec from Canada will necessarily be accompanied by the reduction of its provincial borders in light of historical principles, international law, and common sense. Shaw and Albert argued that the French of Quebec would prefer a large province to a small country. Perhaps they would. We, however, believe that the rest of us would be better off if Quebec were a small country and not a large province. We expect to have friendly relations with Quebec, much as we do with Portugal or Finland or Costa Rica. But we would be finished with the endless disorders caused by a large province that is skewing the real priorities of our nation.

CANADA WITHOUT QUEBEC

The departure of Quebec would provide a magnificent opportunity for Canadians to undertake a genuine restructuring of the political order in which they live. Indeed, the departure of Quebec is the necessary condition for serious thinking about Canada's future as a country. So long as Quebec is part of Canada we will have to deal with Quebec's political problems first. Since those problems are insoluble so long as Quebec is part of Canada, the real problems of the rest of the country will never come to the top of the agenda and will never get dealt with. The expenditure crisis, the deficit crisis, the debt crisis, however you identify it, symbolizes this fact. By going so far into debt we have mortgaged the future, which should have given us a bit of breathing space to deal with the constitution and with Quebec. We blew it. Now the debt is worse and the constitutional position regarding Quebec is worse. The only way to deal with either one is to deal with them both at once. The departure of Quebec may galvanize Canadians to tackle their own real and pressing problems.

It is obviously not up to a couple of university professors to write their nation's constitution. We are willing to give it a try, but nobody has asked us yet. What we can do, even without being asked, is make clear the principles that we believe must guide statesmen and legislators so that they will have a chance, perhaps a last chance, to rescue Canada from paralysis and create a decent liberal democracy across the northern part of the continent. That is the topic for this concluding chapter. What then do we see for Canada? As we are neither fortune tellers nor prophets, it is impossible to answer that question in any definitive way. What follows, therefore, is based on a combination of assumption, reasonable forecasting, hope, and wishful thinking.

Canada without Quebec is a road so far untravelled. But just as Canadians must ready themselves to say "goodbye and good luck" to the French of Quebec, they also need to begin thinking ahead to when Quebec will be a foreign country. If Canadians cannot only reconcile themselves to the coming divorce, but look ahead to life after the marriage, it will make it much easier to survive the crisis days ahead. We believe that, just as in a divorce between two people, the pain of the immediate separation of Quebec from Canada will eventually give way to a determination in both countries to create a new national life on an even more active and vigorous level than before.

We do not presume to suggest to Québécois what sort of independent nation they ought to build. As we have said elsewhere in this book, we assume that the commitment of Québécois to liberal democracy is no less strong than the commitment of Canadians. The current French nationalist fevers in Quebec, we believe, are in large measure a consequence of the constitutional impasse. We have seen that one strain of French thinking has always been wary of accommodation with the rest of the country. Under the present conditions Quebec has been able to disrupt Canadian liberal democracy to such an extent that the legitimacy of the regime itself has been called into doubt. The separation of Quebec will rid Canada of its greatest source of political disorder; the independence of Quebec will also put an end to the need for French nationalist sentiments there. Without

"English" Canada the *raison d'être* of Quebec nationalism dissolves. It is for this reason that we are sanguine regarding post-independence liberal democracy in the State of Quebec. Besides, sandwiched between two larger countries whose societies, economies, and social systems, are liberal-democratic in nature, it would be only prudent for the State of Quebec to follow suit.

In what follows we make several assumptions that are, we believe, not wildly unrealistic. The first is that, after the separation of Quebec, Canadians will indeed want to maintain Canada. It is our belief that economic self-interest, a common historical experience, and emotional ties to the idea of building a unique North American liberal democracy will lead most Canadians to want to keep Canada, despite its new circumstances, much as it is now. We also think that the prospects of building a more united country based on common political and social values will, in fact, appeal to Canadians. Although Canadians will mourn the loss of their Québécois cousins, they will also welcome the opportunity to tackle the difficult economic and social problems that have plagued us for more than a generation but that, as a divided people, we have been unable to address. And after we have begun to come to grips with those challenges, we can also turn our attention to the more universal issues that the twenty-first century will force us to address — trade-offs between economic development and environmental degradation, economic integration, the need for a national educational strategy, the challenge of a world market, the world communications revolution, and so on.

We believe, therefore, that the issue of whether or not there is to be an independent political entity on the northern half of this continent was answered long ago with a resounding yes. Those Canadians who have wanted to be Americans have voted with their feet. The rest have declared, every day, in ways large and small, that they are, and wish to be, Canadians. Unless there are a substantial number of Canadians, native-born or immigrants, whose presence, or belief, in Canada was and is tied to having Quebec remain a part of the national fabric, this will not change. We do not believe there are many such people.

The question is often raised as to how it would be possible for the Atlantic provinces to remain a part of Canada if Quebec is a separate country. The question is based on two false assumptions. The first is that the absence of Quebec would somehow weaken the economic, emotional, and other commitments that Atlantic Canadians have to Canada. But why should it? They have strong ties of trade, transportation, economics, and history with the rest of Canada. Many Atlantic Canadians have family elsewhere in Canada; many have lived and worked in other parts of the country in the past and aspire to do so again in the future. None of that will change with Quebec's departure.

The second assumption on which the question is based is that there will be no geographic contiguity between New Brunswick and Ontario. As we have mentioned earlier, however, this is an assumption too easily made. Since Quebec has no prior claim on the south shore of the St. Lawrence we assume that in the negotiations that would follow Quebec's declaration of independence Canada will secure that territory as part of its geographic boundaries. But even if we are wrong and Canadian negotiators give in to a misguided sense of charity, or to stupidity, or to cowardice (or a combination of all three), they will surely secure the right of free and innocent passage across Quebec in exchange for the right of Quebec ships and aircraft, military and civilian, to free and innocent passage through the St. Lawrence Seaway, the Strait of Belle Isle, and Cabot Strait. The example that is most frequently cited to prove how impossible it would be for the Atlantic provinces to remain part of Canada — failure of Pakistan to survive in two parts — is not relevant. Quebec will be a friendly country sharing mutual interests. A better analogy is the separation of Alaska from the continental United States — an arrangement that works perfectly well.

In any case, the people of the Atlantic provinces would have little choice but to remain in Canada because their present economic weakness would not allow independence and would definitely work against any efforts that might be launched there, or in the United States, to bring about a union with the Great Republic. Thus if Canadians west of the Ontario-Quebec border will have them — and we believe they will — the country will still stretch *A Mari usque ad mare* — from sea to sea — though not, as the rest of Psalm 72 says, from the river to the ends of the earth.

We believe that the departure of Quebec will prompt Canadians to pull together even more in the future than they have in the past because they will have had ample evidence of where rampant provincialism leads. It will, therefore, be necessary to make a number of fundamental changes to the Canadian Constitution. There are plenty of policy options that we would advocate, from eliminating Section 36 of the Constitution, which enshrines the doctrine of equalization of regional disparities, limiting the flexibility of the Bank of Canada, and downsizing the cabinet, to legally limiting the use of the GST to debt reduction. Our concern here, however, is with more fundamental constitutional principles. Three measures in particular are needed to ensure that our new beginning is soundly established.

First, the Constitution ought to indicate in its preamble that it is the sovereign wish of the people of Canada to establish an indissoluble union. Despite the fact that preambles are not the basis for litigation, it would indicate to Canada's political leaders, now and in the future, that the departure of Quebec sets no precedent. It would declare that the more than twenty million Canadians who will be left after Quebec sets out on its own, and the millions more who will come here to live, are partners in a commonwealth of mutual interest. We believe that no self-respecting federation ever allows a part of itself to strike off on its own simply because that part believes independence is to its own advantage. To do so is to admit a principle that puts the entire federal structure in danger. It is like leaving a group that has nurtured and supported you when you believe you can finally do better on your own regardless of what impact your departure might have on those who stay. Put simply, Abraham Lincoln was politically, constitutionally, and morally right to use force to preserve the United States as one union.

How can we reconcile this view with our belief that the best course for Canadians is to accept the separation of Quebec? It is true that all Canadian political leaders, federal or provincial, have rejected the principle of indissolubility. Trudeau was the first to declare that no one would dream of trying to prevent Quebec's departure by force of arms. And since Canadians won't fight to keep Quebec in, we bow to contemporary reality. As well, we believe that the costs of having Quebec in Canada are, and have been, too high anyway, and that far from disadvantaging Canada, Quebec's secession will benefit Canada in the long run. Moreover, the Constitution does not address the secession question, and thus the issue of whether or not a province can secede is political, not constitutional. As we have seen, our political leaders are clearly prepared to allow it under the current regime, and it is impossible to change the rules now. There too we bow to reality. Once Quebec leaves, however, the new federation should be based on the assumption that it will be perpetual. That way Canadians and their political leaders will know that talk of dissolution or separation is beyond the pale of Canadian political and constitutional discussion. The separation bogeyman will be dead.

The second constitutional principle we recommend would declare that Canada constitutes a free market and that the laws of Canada and the provinces are to be interpreted by the courts in a manner consistent with the object of preserving freedom of movement for people and goods within Canada. The time has surely come to make trade between provinces as free as trade with the United States will be when the Canada-United States Free Trade Agreement goes into full effect at the beginning of 1999. Canada's internal barriers against trade and the free movement of peoples have been a significant factor promoting sectionalism over the past 120 years and are simply too inefficient to be acceptable in the last decade of the twentieth century. They must go.

A third constitutional principle concerns individual liberties. The bedrock of liberal democracy, we have said, is that governments are constituted to secure individual freedom. This implies that legislatures are the servants of the people, not the other way around. Popular sovereignty, declared in the preamble to the Constitution, may be institutionalized in articles providing for referenda, citizen initiatives, and the recall of elected members. We are well aware that this would alter fundamentally the structure of Parliament, party discipline, and cabinet control of backbenchers. That is precisely what we wish to do. It is clear to us and, we suspect, to many Canadians that the existing political structure, which puts such a high premium on party discipline, does not serve the interests of Canadian citizens, however much it serves the interests of governments, cabinets and prime ministers. In addition to the new political procedures just mentioned — the recall of MPs, etc. — we would advocate redistributing the seats currently occupied by MPs from Quebec. The result would be smaller constituencies than Canada currently enjoys and, we expect, greater responsiveness on the part of MPs to the interests of their constituents.

Implied in the principle of individual liberty is the abolition of collective rights and legally sustained distinct societies — with a single and partial exception, to be indicated below. Liberal democracies have one class of citizen, not two or three or four.

A fourth constitutional principle would declare that Canada is a true federation. This means that Parliament will be bicameral and that the upper house, the Senate, will represent the population of Canada by territory. The House of Commons will continue, as at present, to represent Canadians in single-member constituencies assigned in approximate proportion to provincial population. In short, we advocate an elected, effective, and equal Senate, a Triple-E Senate.

Senate reform is long overdue in Canada. When the Canadian people elect an upper house that safeguards their regional interests, but does so from a national perspective, Canada will be a more united nation. With Quebec gone, a major obstacle on the road to Senate reform will be removed. Ontario will be outnumbered anyway in the new House of Commons by a combination of western and Atlantic seats (according to the current set-up it would have 99 seats out of 220 after Quebec's 75 MPs leave) and thus one argument often raised against a Triple-E Senate — that although Ontario is the most populous province, its representatives will be outnumbered — will already have been addressed.

Senate reform is not aimed at Ontario in any event. The point of having regional representation in central government institutions is both to ensure that regional interests are made visible in the national capital and to undercut the parochial, one-sided, and, in the invidious sense of the term, provincial articulation of regional demands. This will mean, if not an end to federal-provincial diplomacy, at least a decline in the venomousness with which it is currently conducted. The provincial premiers will be able to concentrate on what they were elected to do — that is, govern their respective provinces. There will be a welcome end to the pretentious posturing that currently goes on at that three-ring circus called a First Ministers' Conference. Executive federalism, as it is called, will be replaced by genuine federalism. Provinces and regions will no longer have to rely on often ill-informed and narrowly focused provincial politicians to make their interests known in the nation's capital. Their elected senators will do it as a full-time job, and they will owe their position not to the whim of a despotic prime minister but to the electors of the region or province that sent them to Ottawa.

The other side of a Triple-E Senate is, of course, that it not be elected on the basis of population. That is the point of a federation: provinces or states or Länder, with vastly different populations, interests, economies, social mores, religious affiliations, and so on, agree to live in the same regime. Those differences are represented *as differences* in the upper house. What they have in common, namely their equality as citizens, is represented in the House of Commons. In other words, the fact that Prince Edward Island or Newfoundland has a much smaller population than British Columbia or Ontario is a reason for an equal number of Senate seats in each province, not a reason to oppose equality. Precisely because it has only four MPs, Prince Edward Island needs equal representation in the Senate. Otherwise its interests can be ignored and its citizens reduced to supplicants and pensioners looking to Ottawa for handouts, which is more or less the current practice.

One of the few bright spots in the entire Meech Lake disaster was the fact that two provinces with small populations were able to prevent a sell-out of the nation to aggressive and ambitious provincial satraps. The purpose of an elected, effective, and equal Senate would be to institutionalize those kinds of checks and balances, rather than leaving them as hostages to fortune. In the Meech Lake example, Canada was very fortunate indeed to have a courageous premier in Newfoundland and a courageous MLA in Manitoba. We would be foolish to assume that our luck will hold. A Triple-E Senate will go some distance to institutionalizing and legitimizing regional political interests.

A Triple-E Senate will also obviate the need for the "notwithstanding" clause of the current Constitution. The original rationale for this clause, namely to provide the provinces with a political remedy against the imposition of federally legislated or judicially imposed uniformity, will no longer be needed. The Senate will ensure that regional divergencies will be accommodated, and the acknowledgement of the principle of popular sovereignty will ensure that no legislature can lightly cancel or suspend individual rights if it believes that such action is in the public interest. It will, on the contrary, make explicit that the highest public interest is the promotion and protection of individual rights.

Not only is there a need for additional provisions to Canada's new constitution, some existing ones will have to go. First and foremost is the provision for official bilingualism. When Canada is a country of more than twenty million people, of whom nineteen million claim English as a mother tongue or working language, official bilingualism will be not just the wasteful extravagance it is now; it will be an anachronism. We have argued that there was never any constitutional need for this policy in the first place; but even if there was the slightest political need for it in the 1960s, that need will have disappeared with Quebec's secession. It will still be both necessary and valuable for Canadians to learn and speak the world's important languages. As part of the general support the federal and provincial governments should give to the education of Canadians, language training and education in French and other languages should continue. But the idea of official languages — any official language, including English, which can take care of itself — must go.

The new Canada emerging after the divorce of Quebec must be a strong democracy with an entrenched Charter of Rights and Freedoms guaranteeing individual liberty as its highest good. It follows, therefore, that we also believe group rights have no place in a true liberal democracy. Rights for individuals? Most definitely. Rights for groups as groups? No, with one exception, which we will discuss shortly. Thus official multiculturalism must go the way of official bilingualism — it must be banished from the Constitution. Canadians of every cultural background must be free to express themselves or conduct themselves as they wish. The degree to which a person assimilates or acculturates should be decided by that person alone. The state must play no role either in forcible assimilation or in creating official, state-sponsored and state-financed incentives for minorities to preserve their culture. If they wish to do so, they must do so for themselves, by themselves.

One final provision will have to come out of the Canadian Constitution: the stipulation establishing or preserving tax-supported separate religious schools in the six out of nine remaining provinces. It is inconsistent in a liberal democracy to provide a special group of citizens, whether Catholic or Protestant or Zoroastrian, with a privilege of tax-supported religious education for their children that other Canadians do not have. Not only is the current system inequitable within those provinces that have separate schools, it creates inequities among Canadians who, because of their religion, enjoy certain privileges in one province, but not in another. Why, for example, should Catholics in Alberta enjoy a right that those in British Columbia do not? They should not. All Canadians should be equal before the law. This is not to say that provincial governments should be prohibited from supporting alternatives to the public-school system. On the contrary. We would like to see the range of choice expanded beyond the usual alternatives of Catholic and non-Catholic. In order to facilitate greater choice, we would advocate, for instance, a flexible voucher system so as to allow parents a greater number of alternatives than are now available. The legitimate interests of the state would be safeguarded by means of provincial education standards and specification of curricula that would have to be met by all alternative or independent schools. Such increased competition would, no doubt, improve the public-school system as well.

There remains one exception to our general principle of citizen equality: Canada's native people. They are not in any sense a minority "ethnic group." For all practical purposes, they are not immigrants; they were Canada's first inhabitants and they entered into direct legal relationships with the Crown under the terms of which they surrendered their aboriginal title to the land in exchange for reserves, cash, and other considerations. Thus, it would be a violation of both law and moral standards to attempt to apply the same legal and constitutional status to them as to other Canadians. We would, in fact, advocate working towards local self-government for native people as one means of ending the institutionalized welfare structure that has kept native people dependent, undermined their pride, and reduced them to second-class citizenship. The exact form of that self-government needs to be defined, but provincial status (within the limits of economic reality) should not be out of the question. The objective of any changes in the constitutional status of native people is to ensure that they are treated equally and that their current status as dependent clients of the state is ended.

It may be asked how this new Canada would differ from the United States in its constitutional, political, and social structures. In our opinion, it would be as different as it is now, except that Canada will have substantially fewer francophones in it. That *would* clearly make Canada more like the United States in one way: the vast majority of Canadians would be English speakers, or would aspire to speak English. Canada will have lost its French-English flavour, and there is no pretending that this will not affect both the way Canadians see themselves and the way others see us. But in other ways, Canada will still be Canada. It will still be a constitutional monarchy with a British parliamentary form of government and laws based on the British experience. The one change, a Triple-E Senate, is a necessity that reflects the geography and history of Canada. Here British experience is not a useful guide. The population mix in English-speaking Canada will be more or less the same. Canadians will still share the unique historical experience of building their own liberal democracy on the northern half of this continent. Our history, the form of our governments, and laws, our population mix, the sparseness of our population, our climate, and our geography have moulded the Canadian character. And they will continue to do so with one major difference — since Canada will have a single political culture it will be more spiritually united even though it will still be spread out geographically. Canadians will still believe in community values, will still feel strongly about crime and gun control and the need to care for each other, whether through state-sponsored and -financed schemes such as medicare or other measures such as voluntary food banks. Those things will not change unless Canadians decide that they must.

The real basis for Canadian independence owes little to the presence or absence of Quebec and a great deal to Canadians' consent to live under a government that ensures that independence. Canadians, in short, have decided to remain independent of the United States not by virtue of their national character or their ethnic diversity or even their historical memory, however important those factors may be. The right of Canada to its independence of the United States (like that of Britain, France, or Venezuela) rests on the right of consent to government. This right, in liberal democracies, is held by individuals, not ethnic groups, "peoples," nations, or religious sects. The guarantee of individual right, as was mentioned in the introduction to this book, is equality before the law — which in turn is a consequence of all human equality. This is what the Americans meant by "inalienable rights." What Canadians share with Americans, at least in this respect, is a commitment to liberal democracy as a regime that is constituted to secure those rights. Such a government, to come full circle, derives its power and authority from the consent of the governed. The logic of liberal democracy, as Harvey Mansfield, Jr., has said, is independent of the logic of national self-determination. Hence the irrelevance of Quebec to the question of liberal democracy in Canada.

Before we leave this discussion of what a new constitutional and political structure might look like, it is important to talk about possible federal-provincial divisions of powers in the new Canada. We do not want to attempt to define in detail which powers we would like to see exercised by the provinces and which by the federal government. For the most part we would be prepared to see the divisions of powers remain more or less as they are at present. Whatever is done in the way of redistributing powers, however, should be done according to one basic principle — just because a division seemed appropriate in 1867 does not mean that it is appropriate now. If there is a role for the federal government in the development of a national educational strategy, for example, then the Constitution should allow it. If there are programs that are best administered by the provinces — day-care might be a good example — then the Constitution should reflect that too.

What sort of relationship should Canada have with the State of Quebec? Assuming that the issues of boundaries, freedom of innocent passage, disposition of federal property, and sharing of national debt can be reasonably resolved — and we assume that they will be — Canada and Quebec should certainly have as close and friendly a relationship as Canada and the United States do now. For instance, it would be entirely appropriate for Canada to enter into negotiations with Quebec aimed at a free-trade agreement. Such an agreement may well prove easier to implement and less contentious than the Canada-United States Free Trade Agreement.

The United States should be invited to join any free-trade discussions that might take place between Quebec and Canada. It might, after all, be interested in open access to the Quebec market, even though that market would amount to less than seven million people (the United States has a free-trade agreement with Israel, a market of less than five million). How the U.S.A. might be able to enter such an agreement with a nation where so much of the basic infrastructure is government subsidized is an open question, but one that will concern the citizens of Quebec, not Canadians. What is clear is that as a secessionist state, Quebec will have no successor rights to the Canada-United States Free Trade Agreement. The Canadian government should make this perfectly plain both to the United States and to the State of Quebec early in the process of negotiation.

There has been much discussion among Quebec separatists about a monetary union with Canada. Canada should consider such a proposal from the State of Quebec, but only under the following conditions: first, representation on the Bank of Canada's advisory board must be on the basis of GDP. Since Canada's GDP is about four times that of Quebec, there will be four Canadians for every Québécois; second, there can be only one governor of the Bank of Canada and he or she must be chosen from the country with the largest GDP; third, there can be only one minister of finance to whom the governor is responsible and he or she will be the minister of the country with the larger GDP. It would go without saying that Canada would have the final say as to whose monetary policy would prevail. On those bases Canada might consider Quebec's use of the Canadian dollar.

This may seem harsh and self-serving, especially when comparisons are made to the coming monetary integration of the EC countries. However, the EC is an agglomeration of twelve countries, several of which are roughly equal in terms of GDP. In that multilateral relationship, something like equality between partners may well be called for. The Canada-Quebec relationship, on the other hand, is bipolar. Because Canada will be, by virtually any measure, roughly 3.5 to 4 times the size of Quebec, Canada's wishes would have to prevail. Should Quebec's GDP ever equal Canada's, the case for full equality will be compelling, but not until then. Why Quebec, as a self-respecting sovereign nation, would accept such conditions is beyond us, but Québécois may believe that their ability to borrow money on the international market will demand the continued use of the Canadian dollar rather than of a purely Quebec currency. (Will they call it the "Lévesque"?) In any event, it would be their decision to initiate the process of restoring economic ties.

Canada, however, might have its own interests in questioning whether economic integration is of benefit. To begin with, Japan, not the United States, is currently the world's largest exporter of finance capital. The Japanese are very much concerned with political stability. It is not clear how attractive to Japanese investors Quebec would be independent of Canada; Canada, in contrast, is likely to appear more attractive without Quebec and the attendant higher costs of doing business in that province. The continued association of Canada and Quebec may well damage Canada's attractiveness without enhancing Quebec's. It is true that the government of Quebec, through its control of pension funds, can direct investment in response to public policy initiatives, but it is also true that government assistance makes the Quebec economy as a whole more vulnerable to declines in the private, tax-generating sector. Here again the benefits of Canadian economic association with Quebec are unclear. In general, therefore, it would be prudent for Canada to take a hard look at the prospect of even minimal economic integration with Quebec.

Other important relationships will have to be established between the two countries. Since environmental pollution knows no boundaries, treaty arrangements will have to be concluded in order to allow both countries to co-operate in limiting and eliminating cross-border pollution. The Canada-United States acid-rain agreements could provide a model. And as Canada and the United States have had long-standing agreements on air defence, the sharing of boundary waters, cross-border air traffic, etc., so too will Canada and Quebec. It will take some time for all these agreements to be put into place — and also for Quebec to develop the appropriate bureaucratic infrastructures to administer them — but eventually, given mutual goodwill, there is no reason to doubt that a comprehensive network of reciprocally satisfactory agreements will govern Canada-Quebec relations.

Obviously this is only a sketch of the basic elements of a Canada-Quebec relationship. Our assumption is that once Canadians discover the silver lining behind the dark cloud of Quebec's secession, they will recover from their hurt (and, possibly, their anger) and realize that their national interest, a shared history, and a common political culture, if nothing else, dictate a close and friendly relationship between the two countries. As sometimes happens in divorce, it is possible that Canada-Quebec relations may be much better when the two nations deal with each other as nations than they were when Quebec was hog-tied into such an unsatisfactory arrangement as Confederation.

More than six-score years ago the people of Quebec and the people of New Brunswick, Nova Scotia, and Ontario created a federal union under the British Crown. Many disparate peoples came together out of self-interest to try to plant the seeds of what would, they hoped, grow into a strong and unique nation. They realized full well that, because of its diverse make-up, Canada would have to be a different sort of country from, for example, the nation states of Europe. And they were acutely aware of the strong determination of Quebeckers to preserve their identity and cultural heritage.

English-speaking Canadians have formed a majority in Canada from the very beginning. Although there have been those among them who have approached Quebec from the perspective of intolerance, bigotry, and racism, the majority — as individuals and through their political leaders — have tried to reach accommodation with Quebec at virtually every turn. Despite their desire to build a nation based on more-or-less commonly agreed-upon ways of doing things and on common goals, they were prepared to accept that unanimity would be a rare thing. Only infrequently did they use raw power to foist their will on Quebec, and not once in the last half century! To balance that, they were prepared to elect a Quebecker as prime minister for approximately thirty out of the last forty-three years, to allow Quebec's post-hoc reservations about the Charlottetown and Victoria agreements of 1964 and 1971 to delay constitutional reform for decades, to accept that Quebec's bloc of MPs in the House of Commons carry far more weight in the making of government policy than the representatives of any other province, and to permit Quebec to receive far more largesse in transfer payments, federal contracts, social assistance, capital expenditures, and so on, than any other province. If Confederation was a business arrangement more than a love-match — and we think it was — Quebec has gained far more from it than it has lost. Quebec today is a strong, confident, vital, energetic, innovative province; as a group, Quebeckers have far more power in Canada than do the people of any other province. Ontario may be the engine of Confederation, but Quebec has firm hold of the steering-wheel.

Despite all this, we in English-speaking Canada have heard mounting threats of secession for the last thirty years. We have responded to those threats with concession after concession until Canada has been brought to the very breaking point. In the spring of 1987 a Canadian prime minister finally proposed to foist a constitutional arrangement on Canada that would have begun the process of dissolving what is left of the ties that bind us and have created two classes of Canadian citizens, those outside Quebec and those within it. To paraphrase Winston Churchill, it might not have been the end, but it would have been the beginning of the end. The people of English-speaking Canada did not know what they wanted for their future, but they did know that Meech Lake was not it.

The death of Meech Lake has brought Quebec nationalism to a fever pitch. Angered that English-speaking Canadians were not prepared to engage in an act of self-immolation, the Quebec nationalists have created a tidal wave of sentiment for radical change in their relationship with Canada. Many clearly believe that dissolving the ties that have bound Quebec to "the English" since 1763 will be a simple matter. Just run the fleur-de-lis up a pole and see who salutes. That is nonsensical self-delusion, but no matter; it is they and they alone who will face that cold, hard reality the morning after. For the rest of us now there can be only one response; we will no more use force to throw you out than we will use force to keep you in. Our reply to your threat of divorce is simple. We say, *"Bon voyage et bonne chance."*

INDEX

aboriginal peoples, 21–22, 29–30, 78, 152, 169–70
Act of Union (1841), 12, 74
Air Canada, 56, 57
Alaska, 162
Albert, Lionel, 156, 157
American Revolution, 70
Atlantic provinces, 154, 162
Atomic Energy *of* Canada Ltd. (AECL), 56

Baldwin, Robert, 74
Bélanger-Campeau Commission, 133
bilingualism, official, 58–60, 80, 119–20, 167–68
Bill of Rights, 117
Bloc Québécois, 21
Borden, Robert L., 32, 87–88, 122
Bouchard, Lucien, 21, 123
Bourassa, Henri, 85–87, 101, 109
Bourassa, Robert, 58, 127–28
Bracken, John, 27, 122
Braid, Don, 134
Brimelow, Peter, 58, 65
British North America Act, 108, 125, 142, 148
Broadbent, Ed, 123, 125, 130
Brossard, Jacques, 139, 154
Brown, George, 75

Caisse de dépôt et placement du Québec, 109, 111
Canada Council, 104
Canada First movement, 80
Canadian government: budgetary his-

tory, 32-34; expenditures of cabinet ministers, 43–51; growth in interventionism, 95; interprovincial trade, 107–08, 164; Keynesian doctrines, 39–42; lack of confidence in, 26–30; liberal democracy, 5–6, 15–16; official bilingualism, 59–60; patriating the constitution, 125–30; provincial secession, 141–42; Quebec Problem, 19–25; regional allocation of net federal fiscal balances, 60–62; regionalism, 51–55; response to Quiet Revolution, 118–25; without Quebec, 157, 159–76
Canadian National (CN), 56
Cartier, George-Etienne, 75, 76
Catholic church, 70–72, 90, 106, 115; Jesuits' Estates Act, 82-83; Manitoba Schools Question, 83-85; tax support for schools, 117, 168–69; Tremblay Commission, 105
Champlain, Samuel de, 68
Chaput, Marcel, 153
Charter of Rights and Freedoms, 117, 118, 129, 168
Chrétien, Jean, 21, 27, 30, 66, 156
Churchill, Winston, 28, 147
citizens in liberal democracy, 6–7
civil service, 49
Clark, Joe, 65, 122
Coleman, William, 105
colonization of North America, 68–70
compensation for opting out, 126, 130